The Angels in Heaven Rejoice

EXPERIENCING *the* FULLNESS *of* YOUR NEW LIFE *in* CHRIST

David CERULLO

THE ANGELS IN HEAVEN REJOICE!

Published by
Inspiration Ministries
P.O. Box 7750
Charlotte, NC 28241

www.inspiration.org

Cover and interior design and composition:
Koechel Peterson & Associates, Inc., Minneapolis, Minnesota

Printed in the United States of America

*This book would not have been possible
without the significant contributions
from my daughter Becky.
Thank you, Becky, for the love you put
into helping me develop this important book
to strengthen and equip new Believers
in their walk with Christ.*

TABLE OF CONTENTS

INTRODUCTION

WELCOME TO THE FAMILY! Did you know that when you accept Jesus as Savior and Lord, all the angels of Heaven throw a party in honor of YOU? It's true! The Bible, God's Word, says that there is rejoicing in the presence of the angels of God over one sinner who gives his life to Jesus (Luke 15:10).

When you ask Jesus to forgive your sins, come into your heart, and be the Lord of your life, you become a "child of God," part of the family of God . . . a Christian.

Christianity is not just another religion. Christianity is a personal relationship with a *living* God! God is real. He is alive, and He loves you very much.

Because He loves and knows you, He wants *you* to know and love *Him.* That's why He has given you the Bible . . . to help you develop a relationship with Him. For this reason, the Bible is the most important Book you will ever read.

As God's personal Word to *YOU,* you will discover that the Bible is full of rich, wonderful truths to help you live successfully in this life and in the life to come. I encourage you to read for yourself what the Bible has to say to you. As you read God's Word and your relationship with Him grows stronger, your understanding of Him and His Word will also grow.

I have written *The Angels in Heaven Rejoice* as a simple explanation of what it means to be a Christian. This is basically a guidebook to help you learn and understand how to live as a Christian. In it, I share with you some of the important building blocks of your new faith and the awesome privileges that come with your decision to follow Christ.

I pray that *The Angels in Heaven Rejoice* equips you with practical insights for developing a personal relationship with God as you choose to walk with Him for the rest of your life.

David

SECTION ONE

WELCOME
to the
FAMILY!

CHAPTER ONE

The Great Exchange

God loves you so much

that He sent His only Son,

Jesus Christ, to earth

in the form of a man

to pay the penalty

for your sins and the sins

of the entire world.

GOD OFFERS US A GIFT, the opportunity to make a "Great Exchange." He offers to exchange our sinfulness for His holiness, to exchange our sickness for His healing, to exchange our eternal death for His eternal life. This Great Exchange is a free gift He offers to every person.

When God created mankind in His own image, He made us perfect. He created us to have a relationship and perfect fellowship with Him.

God never intended for us to get sick. He never intended for us to sin. He never intended for us to die. But something happened that changed all that. Sadly, the first man and woman He ever created, Adam and Eve, made a choice to disobey God.

You know from your own life experiences that there are always consequences to your actions, choices, and decisions. And the consequences of Adam and Eve's decision to disobey God brought sin, sickness, and death into the world. The Bible says that the wages (the reward, the compensation) for sin is *death* (Romans 6:23).

WITHOUT GOD, WE ARE WITHOUT HOPE!

Because Adam and Eve decided to disobey God, all of us are born separated from Him. Their decision to sin condemns us all to physical and spiritual death for eternity.

The Bible teaches that each one of us is separated from God by our own stubbornness and sin. Because of this, we truly are without hope and without God. We deserve to suffer eternal death as the punishment for our sinfulness.

Yet, despite what we deserve, God loves us so much that He made a plan to bring us back into fellowship and to restore our relationship with Him. The plan is simple: God sent His perfect Son, Jesus Christ, to earth as a man to be punished for our sins in our place.

Jesus came as a baby born to a virgin by the power of the Holy Spirit. He lived a sinless life and then died a torturous death by being nailed to the Cross and allowed to hang there until He died. While Jesus was on the Cross, the judgment for the sins of the whole world were laid upon Him, and God, in His holiness, had to turn away from Jesus as He was crucified. But then wonderfully, miraculously, God raised Jesus from the dead after He had been buried for three days!

When you believe that Jesus is God's Son and that He was punished for your sins in your place; when you believe that God raised Him from the dead; when you accept Jesus as your Savior and make Him the Lord of your life; and when you choose to walk in obedience to God and His Word, then you receive the right to spend a glorious eternity in Heaven with Him!

You exchange your will for His. You exchange eternal condemnation without Him for eternity in Heaven with Him. You exchange a life of fear, anxiety, and worry for a life filled with His peace beyond our human ability to understand (Philippians 4:7).

PAYING THE RANSOM

If a dearly loved child were to be kidnapped, the desperate parents would pay any price asked by the kidnapper to free their stolen child. They would pay a "ransom," which is a payment made in order to free something precious that has been stolen.

Well, as far as God is concerned, we are His creation, and we have been kidnapped! We are victims of His enemy, Satan, who has stolen and intends to hold us as his captives, bound by the chains of our own sin. We can't set ourselves free, and we can't pay the ransom. We are completely helpless, trapped by Satan and our own sinful nature!

God could have left us in His enemy's hands. He could have been content to just create us and then leave us alone to fend for ourselves. But He so desires to have a close relationship with us that He sent His Son to set us free. This is what distinguishes us from the animals He created. He doesn't just want us to be His *creatures* . . . He wants us to be His **children,** walking in a loving relationship with their Father.

The good news is that Jesus Christ, God's Son, paid the price for our freedom with His own Blood so that we could be God's children. By His death on the Cross, Jesus paid the ransom for your life and mine. Even though our sin condemns us, He died in our place to set us free and satisfy the sentence of eternal death that we deserve. When we accept Him as our Savior and Lord, we are ransomed and set free from our sins and from Satan's chains!

GET OUT OF JAIL FREE!

Imagine you are locked in prison, convicted of crimes you are guilty of committing. You have been sentenced to death and are waiting on death row for your execution. Suddenly, you learn that someone has offered to take your place on death row and to be executed in your place.

Would you choose to stay behind bars and await execution? Of course not! You would be thrilled to be set free! You would go running out of that prison and never look back!

Well, this is what happens when you become a Christian. Even though you are on "death row" awaiting the execution you deserve, Jesus offers you a "Get Out of Jail Free" card! You can escape the prison of your sins and never look back, except to thank the One who has delivered you from eternal death!

There's a chorus that says, "We had a debt we could not pay; He paid a debt He did not owe." We can't pay the price to redeem ourselves because God doesn't recognize any of our efforts to remove our own sin. Why? Because Isaiah says in the Bible, *"For all of us have become like one who is unclean, and all our righteous deeds are like a filthy garment"* (Isaiah 64:6).

The word "righteous" means having "right standing" before God. None of us is righteous on our own. We cannot stand before God and defend, excuse, or justify our sinful behaviors and thoughts. But God's Word declares, *"He made Him who knew no sin to be sin on our behalf,*

that we might become the righteousness of God in Him"
(2 Corinthians 5:21).

THE SIMPLICITY OF THE GOSPEL

The story of the Gospel is simple. It's admitting that
you need a relationship with the God who made you. It's
accepting God's judgment that you are guilty of sin as
charged. It's facing the truth that you are helpless to save
yourself or set yourself free from your sins.

It's acknowledging that God's solution to your sinfulness is the ONLY answer: Jesus Christ. It's recognizing that
when you invite Him to come into your life, forgive your
sins, and be the Lord of your life, your sins and God's sentence of death are transferred from you to Christ. And in
this Great Exchange, you transfer your trust from your
ability to save yourself to trusting Christ *alone.*

When you invite Christ to be the Lord of your life,
you are inviting Him to have authority over *every* area of
your life. By exchanging His righteousness for your sin,
you inherit His salvation. "Salvation" means to be set free,
to be delivered, protected, healed, and made whole from
sin, sickness and death.

HAVE YOU MADE THE GREAT EXCHANGE?

Perhaps you've already made the most important
decision of your entire life . . . the decision to invite Jesus
Christ into your life . . . to forgive your sins . . . and to be
the Savior and Master of your life.

On the other hand, if you haven't received God's free gift of salvation . . . if you haven't invited Him to be your Lord . . . if you haven't made this Great Exchange with God, you can!

How? It's simple. The Bible says, *"If you confess with your mouth Jesus as Lord, and believe in your heart that God raised Him from the dead, you will be saved. For with the heart a person believes, resulting in righteousness, and with the mouth he confesses, resulting in salvation"* (Romans 10:9-10).

You see, it's not your way or my way. It must be God's way. Jesus says, *"I am the way, and the truth, and the life; no one comes to the Father, but through me"* (John 14:6).

CHOOSE WHOM YOU WILL SERVE

The Bible says that we can't even come to Jesus unless God, our Heavenly Father, helps us to come to Him (John 6:44-65). If you have never invited Jesus to be your Savior and Lord, that pull you may be feeling in your heart right now, that desire to fill the emptiness in your life, is God's Holy Spirit drawing you to Jesus Christ.

God loves you so much! He has so many wonderful blessings, promises, and gifts He wants to share with you. He has chosen you to be a part of His Family forever. But you must choose *Him*. He will not make up your mind for you, nor will He force Himself on you. If there were 100 steps between you and God, He would take 99, but He would leave that last step to you.

He has given you a free will so that you can make your own choices. You must choose whom you will serve . . . yourself or God. Will you ask Jesus to be your Lord? Will you make the decision today, right now, to give Him authority over *every* area of your life? When you choose God and His Son, then you will be able to experience His Power, Presence, and Peace in your life.

THE GREATEST MIRACLE

If you would like to experience the greatest miracle in all the world . . . the miracle of salvation . . . you can right now. Simply invite Jesus to come into your life and forgive you for all of your sins. Ask Him to wipe away your past and be the Lord and Master of your life. Then choose to believe in your heart that God raised Jesus from the dead. It's that simple.

Would you pray this prayer with me right now?

Dear Jesus,

I know that I am a sinner. Please forgive me for my sins and wash my heart clean. Thank You for dying on the Cross for me.

The Bible says that if I confess with my mouth and believe in my heart that You are Lord, then I will be saved. Jesus, I believe that You are Lord and that God raised You from the dead.

Please come and live in my heart. Be the Lord of my life. Teach me to walk with You and live for You for the rest of my life. Thank You for saving my life and giving me the opportunity to live eternally in Heaven with You. Amen.

If you just prayed that prayer and now believe in Jesus as your Savior, you are "born again" into a new life and you are saved by God's amazing grace! The angels in heaven literally are rejoicing right now over **YOU** and your salvation! Welcome to the Family of God!

I am so glad you have made the decision to follow Christ. With that simple prayer, your name is now written in a special book, which the Bible calls *The Lamb's Book of Life*. This is a book containing all the names of those who have accepted Christ into their hearts (Revelation 3:5). God Himself has written your name in His book, forever confirming your salvation! You are now a child of God!

GOD'S PLAN FOR YOUR LIFE

The Bible says, *"For You formed my inward parts; You wove me in my mother's womb. I will give thanks to You, for I am fearfully and wonderfully made"* (Psalm 139:13-14). God loves you so much! He has designed a special plan for your life.

The plan God has for your life is to prosper you and not to harm you in any way. His plan is to give you a future and a hope (Jeremiah 29:11). God has great things in store for you!

As you begin your new life with Him, this great adventure, this exciting journey, I encourage you to spend time with Him. Talk to Him. Sit quietly and listen for His voice to speak to you.

Reading your Bible every day helps you learn to recognize His voice. Referring to Himself as a Shepherd leading His sheep, Jesus says, *"The sheep follow him because **they know his voice"*** (John 10:4). To recognize His voice, you need to become familiar with His Word.

As you grow and mature in your new faith and in your knowledge of the Bible, you will learn to hear the Lord's voice in your mind and heart. He will bring you tremendous comfort and direction for your life as your understanding of Scripture increases.

As you learn to recognize His voice, God will begin to reveal His plans and purposes for your life. Don't be afraid of what the Lord has in store for you. God's plan for your life is exciting and good!

DON'T BE OVERWHELMED!

God is not going to show you every plan for your life all at once. He says that His Word will be a lamp to your feet and a light to your path (Psalm 119:105). This means that the Lord will shine the light of His love and the light of His Word into your life and reveal just what you need to know in order to take the next step. You must learn to *trust* Him day-by-day, moment-by-moment. This is *faith.*

Faith simply is responding in obedience to what you

believe is God's will for your life. You will not always be 100% accurate in your understanding of what He is saying to you, especially in the beginning of your new walk with Him. But that's OK. Just the fact that you *want* to obey Him and are trying to hear His voice pleases Him!

Your new life with God in control and Jesus as your Lord will be a daily pilgrimage, a step-by-step journey that you are traveling. As you draw near to God, the Bible says that He will draw near to you (James 4:8). He will lead you where He wants you to go, one step at a time. Take courage in knowing that God's plan for you is best and that His ways are always right. Trust His hand to guide you.

THE POTTER'S HANDS

God knows your heart. In fact, He knows you better than you know yourself. So, it's important that you learn to trust God and allow Him to shape your life.

This truth is illustrated in the Bible when God speaks to a man named Jeremiah. God tells Jeremiah to go to the potter's house, and Jeremiah obeys God.

When he arrives, he sees the potter working at his potter's wheel. But the clay he is shaping becomes damaged, so the potter begins forming a different pot. The Lord then spoke to Jeremiah and says, *"Behold, like the clay in the potter's hand, so are you in My hand"* (Jeremiah 18:6).

It is impossible for clay to take shape without the potter. Clay has no purpose in and of itself. It cannot take form or shape or achieve the potter's design and purpose for it until the potter has molded and shaped it.

Even after the clay is molded into the potter's plan for it, the clay still must remain in his hands to fulfill its purpose. If the potter makes the clay into a pitcher, it cannot draw water on its own. The potter is the one who must fill the pitcher up and pour the water out.

There is a wonderful hymn written in 1907 by Adelaide Pollard called, *"Have Thine Own Way Lord."* Here are some of the words to this great classic:

> *"Have Thine own way, Lord, have Thine own way;*
> *Thou art the Potter, I am the clay.*
> *Mold me and make me after Thy will,*
> *While I am waiting, yielded and still.*
> *Have Thine own way, Lord, have Thine own way,*
> *Hold over my being, absolute sway.*
> *Fill with Thy Spirit, till all shall see*
> *Christ only, always living in me."*

Doesn't it make sense to yield to the Creator who designed you? Like clay in the potter's hands, you must be moldable in His hands. Trust God, and as the Bible says, *"He who began a good work in you will perfect it (complete it or bring it to maturity) until the day of Christ Jesus"* (Philippians 1:6).

"The day of Christ Jesus" is the day when Jesus will return to earth to take His followers home to be with Him in Heaven. And what a glorious day that will be!

(Note: If you don't already have a Bible, I encourage you to get one right away. Any bookstore sells Bibles. Ask for a modern translation, which can be easier to understand. When you start reading your Bible, I suggest that you start in the book of John in the New Testament. This book will teach you a lot about who Jesus Christ is and what your new life with Him will be like!)

CHAPTER TWO

This New Road

*H*ave you heard people

use words like "born again"

or "saved"? These words

may not make sense to you

as a new Christian.

TO BE "BORN AGAIN" DOES NOT MEAN that you experience a second physical birth! Being born again speaks of a *spiritual* birth. Your new life begins as you start your walk with Christ. When you pray and ask God to forgive your sins and for Jesus to be the Lord of your life, you start that new life!

There was a man in the Bible who had a hard time understanding this truth. His name was Nicodemus, and he was a Jewish leader in Jesus' day.

When Nicodemus comes to Jesus with questions, Jesus tells him,

> "*Unless one is born again, he cannot see the kingdom of God.*

> "*Nicodemus said to Him, 'How can a man be born when he is old? He cannot enter a second time into his mother's womb and be born, can he?'*

> "*Jesus answered, 'Truly, truly, I say to you unless one is born of water and the Spirit, he cannot enter into the kingdom of God. That which is born of the flesh is flesh, and that which is born of the Spirit is spirit*"(John 3:3-6).

Jesus was explaining a *spiritual birth*. When you are born again, God's Holy Spirit breathes new life into your spirit. Christ is then born in you *spiritually*.

Paul, a follower of Christ and a powerful leader in the early Christian Church, describes this concept when he says, "*Christ **in** you, the hope of glory*" (Colossians 1:27).

When you ask Christ to come into your heart, He

gives you a fresh start in life. In fact, the Bible even calls you a "new creation":

"If any man is in Christ, he is a new creation, the old has gone and behold, God has made all things new!" (2 Corinthians 5:17). The Spirit of God Himself has now come to live inside your heart. This is the mystery and wonder of the Gospel!

This new life you have begun as a Christian is similar to your natural birth. In fact, there is a great parallel between a newborn baby in a physical sense and a newborn baby in the spiritual sense.

When a child is born, several things need to happen for him to survive and grow. A baby must be fed and nourished. Without food and nourishment, he would soon starve.

A baby is dependent upon his parents for the basic necessities of life. He cannot care for himself. Someone has to feed and cloth him. Someone has to love and shelter him. A baby needs loving arms to hold him close so he feels comforted and safe.

A baby needs a gentle voice singing to soothe his fears. Without care, a neglected baby can not survive. A baby must also receive love. Doctors say that without affection, babies tend to withdraw and even lose the will to live. In short, babies are very fragile.

When a baby is born, he doesn't begin talking and walking and caring for himself on day one. No, it takes time for the baby to grow and mature and learn.

SPIRITUAL NOURISHMENT

These same parallels can be made to a newborn spiritual life. A "baby" Christian needs food, shelter, clothing, warmth, caring and loving in the spiritual sense. Spiritual maturity doesn't take place overnight any more than physical maturity takes place overnight. It takes time.

How does a newly "born again" person receive spiritual nourishment? By reading God's Word and obeying it. Just as a newborn baby must be fed often in order to thrive and grow, so must you feed your spirit so that you will thrive and grow as a Christian. The Bible is the bread of life, and its words are food for your soul! When you read the Bible, pray and ask God to help you understand His words to you.

Your spirit will also be fed by spending time talking with God and worshipping Him. In addition, you need to fellowship with other Christians in a Bible-believing church or study group that believes in the truth of the *whole* Bible. Within a community of Believers, you will find love, support, protection and shelter. While the Church is far from perfect, it is God's design that you grow in community with His children.

Every day is a learning experience for a child, with many new objects, faces, sounds, colors and movements. He encounters new foods and places, words and ideas. A child learns that life is a process of growing and learning.

All these principles apply to the spiritual world as well. Your new life and your relationship with Christ is a process of growing and learning. Your relationship with Him will mature and deepen with every lesson and experience you encounter.

THE JOURNEY

Remember, your relationship with God is a journey. It is a process of learning and growing into all that He has designed for your life. As you find yourself spending more time with the Lord, you will discover that you are being transformed more and more into His perfect image. This is the primary goal of a Christian . . . to become more and more like our Savior, Jesus Christ. As you take the time to get to know Him, like the potter with the clay, He will mold you into the image of His Son.

Your life will be a journey of high points and low points. There will be times when you follow God's Word and times when you fail to follow His Word. Even the great men and women of the Bible struggled with sin at times in their lives.

Paul talked about a war waging inside his body and his struggle to do what was right versus what was wrong. And he did not always choose to do the right thing. He said in Romans 7:18, *For the willing [to do good] is present in me, but the doing of the good is not."* When you get a moment, read the whole chapter of Romans 7 to help you understand the battle that rages between your and God's righteousness, and between your flesh and your spirit.

Living for Christ does not make you perfect. But the more you grow in your relationship with God, the easier it will be to trust Him and rely on His grace to see you through times of temptation and testing. Despite his struggles, Paul could say with full confidence, *"Thanks be to God, who always leads us in triumph in Christ"* (2 Corinthians 2:14).

Even when you struggle or fail (and we all do!), God's heart is always to restore us and set us back on the right path.

SWEET SURRENDER

You will find that one of the most important things you can do is to recommit your life to Christ every day. In Romans 12:1, the Apostle Paul wrote that Christians are to *"present your bodies a living and holy sacrifice, acceptable to God."* This means that you learn to daily surrender your will and your decision-making to Him. This is what it means for Jesus to be in control of your life. When you live with Jesus as Lord, you finally discover the true meaning of joy and peace!

The book of Proverbs (written by King Solomon) gives us this practical advice to help us yield our lives to the Lord: *"Trust in the LORD with all your heart and do not lean on your own understanding. In all your ways acknowledge Him, and He will make your paths straight"* (Proverbs 3:5-6).

As you begin yielding your life to Christ more and more, you will find His Holy Spirit becoming more evident in your life. When you come up against a temptation or a trying circumstance, you will discover that your fleshly desires are diminishing and that God's Spirit is active in your life.

This is 2 Corinthians 3:18 at work. This verse states, *"We are being transformed into the Lord's likeness with ever increasing glory."* The word "glory" means splendor, honor, and magnificence, and God will take your life from glory to glory to glory until one precious day, you will be standing in Heaven with Jesus completely transformed into His glorious image!

YOUR INHERITANCE!

Now that you have accepted Jesus into your heart as your Lord and Savior, you have become a child of God. Galatians 4:6-7 says, *"Because you are sons, God has sent the Spirit of His Son into our hearts, crying 'Abba, Father.' Therefore you are no longer a slave, but a son; and since you are a son, God has also made you an heir through Jesus."*

The word *Abba* is Hebrew for "daddy." God has adopted you into *His* kingdom and into *His* family as *His* child. You have inherited eternal life with Him. Wow! What an awesome privilege!

An heir is a person who is entitled to receive property, possessions, or benefits from someone who wants to give something special to that person. Our children will inherit whatever we choose to leave them after our time here on earth is over. We make them our heirs because we love them and want to bless them.

As God's child, you are now entitled to all the blessings and benefits of being a part of His family. God has made you a *"joint heir with Jesus Christ"* (Romans 8:17).

What have you inherited? First and most importantly, you have inherited eternal life. Your sins have been forgiven. Heaven is your destination. As His child, you have also inherited all of the promises of Scripture as yours *right now!*

As you walk in close relationship with Him, you have the promise of His Presence, Peace, and Provision. You are entitled to His joy, patience, and comfort. As His child you have the right to go to Him at any time to talk to Him or just be with Him. And when you die, you inherit an eternity of living in Heaven with Him . . . an inheritance that no one can ever take from you!

Do you understand that this inheritance, these gifts and blessings, are only for God's **children?** Those who do not choose to believe in Jesus Christ as their Savior and Lord are *not* God's heirs. Therefore, they are not entitled to His Presence, Peace, or Prosperity! These blessings are reserved as an inheritance for God's sons and daughters ONLY!

LIFE WON'T ALWAYS BE EASY

Just because you now are a child of God and entitled to the Kingdom of Heaven does not mean your life on this earth is going to be perfect and easy. Even when you are trusting God with all of your heart, there still will be difficult times. The Bible says that the sun shines on the evil and the good, and that the rain falls on the righteous and the unrighteous (Matthew 5:45). There still will be rainy days and hard times in your life.

"So what's the point in believing?" you may ask. Well, now that you are a Christian, when these hard times come, you can count on a Faithful Companion who will *never leave you nor forsake you*" (Hebrews 13:5). You will never be alone again!

God will always give you the strength you need to make it through any adversity. His strength is made perfect in your weakness (2 Corinthians 12:9). In the book of Isaiah, God speaks to us saying, *"Do not fear, for I am with you; do not anxiously look about you, for I am your God. I will strengthen you, surely I will help you, surely I will uphold you with My righteous right hand"* (Isaiah 41:10).

What could you or I possibly have to worry about with the Creator of this incredible universe on our side? When you have a problem that is weighing heavily on your heart, just give it to God. The Bible says, *"Cast your burden upon the LORD, and He will sustain you; He will never allow the righteous to be shaken"* (Psalm 55:22).

Whether the situation is big or small, God cares. He cares about every detail in your life. He even has the number of hairs on your head counted (Matthew 10:30)!

BE ENCOURAGED

You are so special to God. No detail in your life is too

small for Him to care about, and no problem is too big for Him to handle. Scripture says, *"God is able to do immeasurably more than all we can ask or imagine, according to the power that is at work within us"* (Ephesians 3:20). I know that I can imagine great things, and this verse assures me that my God is able to do far more than you or I can imagine!

When it feels like the foundation of your life is on sinking sand, take courage. In Matthew 7:24-27, Jesus describes a storm that assaulted a man whose life was built on a firm foundation. Jesus says, *"The rain came down, the streams rose, and the winds blew and beat against the house; yet it did not fall, because it had its foundation on the rock."* In Jesus Christ you now have a solid Rock on which you can firmly stand.

When the winds of calamity blow in, relax. You now have a shelter in the midst of the storm. *"God is a refuge for the poor, a refuge for the needy in distress a shelter in the storm and a shade from the heat"* (Isaiah 25:4).

If you are feeling deserted and in despair, take heart. Proverbs 18:24 declares *"A man of many companions may come to ruin, but there is a friend that sticks closer than a brother."* Jesus is your best friend, and He will stick closer to you than a brother.

WHO IS GOD?

The Bible, particularly in the Old Testament, uses several names to describe God. The following verses give us a clearer understanding of His nature:

If financial strains and pressures seem overwhelming, know that God is your *"Jehovah-Jirah,"* which means "God our Provider." He is on your side!

If sickness, disease or pain overshadows you or your family, you are entitled to a second opinion from the Great Physician. He is *"Jehovah-Rapha,"* which means "the Lord our Healer." Isaiah declared, *"He was wounded for our transgressions, He was bruised for our iniquities: the chastisement of our peace was upon Him; and with His stripes we are healed"* (Isaiah 53:5).

If you are trapped in a lifestyle or habit that has you enslaved to its desire, there is hope because God is *"the strength of my salvation"* (Psalm 140:7).

If depression, tragedy, or loneliness leaves your heart feeling broken and weary, please know that God is able to comfort you. Second Corinthians 1:3 declares, *"Praise be to the God and Father of our Lord Jesus Christ, the Father of compassion and the God of all comfort, who comforts us in all our troubles so that we can comfort those in any trouble with the comfort we ourselves received from God."* He is our *"Jehovah-Shalom,"* which means, "The Lord is our peace."

God is able to fill you with a supernatural joy that will be your strength. *"The joy of the Lord is your strength"* (Nehemiah 8:10).

When you need wisdom, direction, and guidance, you can simply ask God and He will give it to you (James 1:5).

If there is something you do not understand, take comfort in knowing that *"The Holy Spirit will teach you all things"* (John 14:26).

If life seems hectic and stressful, trust in God. Isaiah 26:3-4 states, *"You will keep in perfect peace him whose mind is steadfast, because he trusts in you. Trust in the Lord forever, for the Lord, the Lord is the Rock eternal."*

When hard times come, and they will, know that God gives a peace that surpasses our human understanding. Philippians 4:6-7 says, *"Be anxious for nothing, but in everything by prayer and supplication with thanksgiving let your requests be made known to God. And the peace of God, which surpasses all comprehension, will guard your hearts and your minds in Christ Jesus."*

AN ETERNAL PERSPECTIVE

I encourage you to always maintain an "eternal perspective." Having an eternal perspective means not living for just the moment and the difficulties it may hold. No, as Believers, we live with the end in sight . . . knowing that one day Jesus Christ will return for us to take us to our heavenly home. How glorious it will be for Believers when we finally see Him face to face!

Because of this, when hardships come, we can say with Paul, *"For I consider that the sufferings of this present time are not worthy to be compared with the glory that is to be revealed to us"* (Romans 8:18).

No matter what the situation is in which you find yourself, God is able to meet you at your point of need! He is sufficient for you; in good times and in hard times God will be your strength. Even if it feels that He is all you have, rest assured knowing He is all you need!

GOD IS IN CONTROL

All of these promises from the Bible provide us with great hope. We may read them and get encouraged or excited as we feel our faith begin to grow inside of us. However, sometimes God's promises can so easily be forgotten as the pressures of life begin to close in on us.

When you are faced with decisions or trials in your life, you now have a new way to approach them. Instead of taking matters into your own hands and facing your problems with your limited strength, trust in God and look to Him first.

I know this is not easy! It can seem much more natural handling life on your own. For years you have been used to dealing with problems alone; you may feel in control that way. But the truth is that you do not know what is best for your life. God has the advantage of knowing the end of your life from the beginning. The outcome of our difficult circumstances is so much better when we pause and look to God for supernatural wisdom, guidance, and direction.

You have the Creator of this amazing universe on your side. He knows all things and has made all things. What awesome privileges you are entitled to as a child of God, a Christian! He loves you more that you will ever understand here on earth. He has adopted you into His Kingdom and made you His child.

He is always with you to help you, guide you, teach you, comfort you, and give you peace, joy, patience, and strength. Whatever you need, God's grace and provision will provide. This sure sounds like an exciting, abundant life, doesn't it?

Soon you will be wondering how you ever lived without the Lord. Not only will you reap benefits in this life on earth, but you will also store up for yourself treasures in Heaven where you will one day live with your Savior forever!

CHAPTER THREE

Why Jesus Had to Die on the Cross

You may wonder
why Jesus had to die
for us so that we could be
forgiven and have eternal life.
I know I often have wished
there were another way
for Jesus to save us,
but there was not.
How grateful I am
to Him for laying down
His own life for me!

WHEN GOD CREATED THIS WORLD, it was perfect and without blemish or sin. Adam and Eve lived in the Garden of Eden and walked with the Lord daily. There was no sickness, no pain, and no death.

God gave Adam and Eve a free will, the ability to choose for themselves what they wanted to do. God does not create puppets. He wants His children to serve Him and obey His guidelines because they love Him. God had given Adam and Eve full reign over His creation with one command. God told Adam not to eat of the tree of the knowledge of good and evil (Genesis 2:17).

FORBIDDEN FRUIT

In Genesis 3:1, Satan came to Eve in the form of a serpent and asked, *"Indeed, has God said, 'You shall not eat from any tree of the garden?' Eve responded and said, 'From the fruit of the trees of the garden we may eat; but from the fruit of the tree which is in the middle of the garden, God said, "You shall not eat from it or touch it, or you will die."'"*

Then Satan lied to Eve and told her God didn't mean what He had said. *"You surely will not die!"* He told her that if she ate the fruit, *"you will become like God, knowing good and evil."* The devil convinced Eve that she would be equal with God and urged her to go ahead and eat the fruit.

As a new Believer, you need to be aware of the devil's strategies. He did not tell Eve outright to disobey God. He introduced doubt about God's integrity and His goodness. From there, it was a short step to disobedience. We'll talk more about temptation later in the book, but I want to encourage you now to guard your mind and heart against doubt and unbelief.

Eve believed the lie and gave into the temptation. Then, instead of honoring God and protecting his wife, Adam disobeyed God and ate the forbidden fruit as well. As a result of their disobedience sin was brought into this world.

God never intended for His creation to experience the effects of sin, but He did want them to have a free will and be capable of making their own decisions.

God didn't create Adam and Eve to be puppets. He didn't want them to worship and obey Him because they had strings attached to them that He could pull and say, "Now it's time to worship Me!" No, He wanted them to worship Him because they chose to.

When Adam and Eve used their free will to disobey God, sin came into this world. So did sickness, sadness, evil, and even death. And not only did physical death come into the world, but more importantly, spiritual death and eternal separation from God became the end for all those who do not know Christ as their Savior and Lord.

THE SHEDDING OF BLOOD

Because of their sin, Adam and Eve could no longer be in God's Presence, so He cast them out of the garden. Time went on and generations passed. But God had a plan!

God planned that a day would come when in His divine timetable, He would send His perfect Son to this earth to die so that by His Blood, God could forgive our sins. I don't know why God established the shedding of blood as the method for the forgiveness of sins, but He did.

Hebrews 9:22 tells us, *"Almost all things are by the law purged with blood; and without shedding of blood there is no forgiveness."* Simply put, sin brought death; life is in the blood, so spiritual life is restored by a blood sacrifice. In Jesus' case, the sacrifice accomplishes our salvation— once and for all for those who believe.

The only way for us to be reconciled to God is by a blood sacrifice to make atonement for our wrongs committed. "Atonement" means "to cover" or "to cleanse." When we sin, a simple "I'm sorry" is not enough. God's justice must be served so that sin can be covered and cleansed.

OFFERING BLOOD SACRIFICES

From the earliest books in the Old Testament, the people of God were given very specific guidelines on how to offer animal sacrifices to God to atone for their sins. God established a Covenant with them—a holy, irrevocable promise—that if they offered the blood sacrifice of animals in atonement for their sins, He would forgive them. Their offerings had to cost them something; they had to be a true sacrifice.

There were many types of sacrifices offered to God for many different purposes. Some were for the cleansing of sin; others were burnt offerings signifying dedication to God. And there were even sacrifices of fellowship offerings.

This idea of offering animal sacrifices can be strange to modern society; nevertheless this was what God established. But ultimately, there was no sacrifice that could possibly be substantial enough to fully pay for our sin.

The process of daily sacrifices and offerings to God went on for hundreds of years. But Scripture tells us the Covenant was insufficient to atone for sin: *"For if that first covenant had been faultless, then no place would have been sought for a second. Finding fault with them, He says: 'Behold, the days are coming, says the Lord, when I will make a **new covenant** with the house of Israel and with the house of Judah'"* (Hebrews 8:7-8).

A NEW COVENANT

Out of His great love and mercy, God was willing to establish a New Covenant. God Himself would pay the highest cost and make the ultimate sacrifice. He would send His one and only Son, Jesus, to the world. Jesus came to take on the sin of the entire world. With His perfect, precious Blood spilled on the Cross of Calvary, He died our death and paid our debt.

Jesus became the final sacrifice to God. His task was not a simple one. He had to leave behind His home in Heaven, come to earth, and take on flesh and blood in the form of a man. Then He had to die one of the most painful and torturous deaths imaginable. Even moments before the soldiers came to take Jesus away to be crucified, He wondered if somehow there was another way.

Beyond the physical pain was the knowledge that the sins of the whole world were going to be on Him. He knew that sin separates us from God, and the thought that He would be separated from His Heavenly Father for those hours on the Cross was almost unbearable. He prayed and asked His Father if there was some way for Him to avoid the suffering and humiliation of the Cross. But He concluded His prayer, saying, *"yet not what I will, but what Thou wilt"* (Mark 14:35-36).

I am so grateful that Jesus yielded to His Father's will. Had he not yielded, we would still be bound by our sin and without hope. The Apostle Paul wrote, *"Very rarely will anyone die for a righteous man, though for a good man someone might possibly dare to die. But God demonstrated his own love for us in this: while we were still sinners, Christ died for us"* (Romans 5:7-8).

As Jesus hung on the Cross, darkness fell over the earth as Jesus literally took the sins of the world (both the penalty and the shame) upon Himself. Since God cannot look upon sin, Jesus felt His Father's Presence leave. In that moment of agonizing separation between Jesus and the Father, He cried out in anguish, *"My God, My God, why have You forsaken Me?"* (Matthew 27:46-54.)

And then it was finished. Jesus had paid OUR ransom with HIS own Blood when He died on that cruel Cross. What a great price Jesus paid for our sins! God loves us so much that He was willing to sacrifice His own dear Son so that we could spend eternity with Him in Heaven.

I encourage you to read Hebrews 8 and 9 to learn more about the priesthood of Christ and the Covenant He made with us through the shedding of His Blood.

A TORN CURTAIN

In Jesus' day, the Jews gathered to worship God in the Temple in Jerusalem. Inside the Temple, there was a great curtain separating the inner and outer courts of the Temple from the Holy of Holies.

The Holy of Holies was where the high priest sprinkled the blood from the animal sacrifices on the altar of God on behalf of himself and the people as the atonement for their sins. Not just anyone could enter this holy place, because the Presence of God dwelt there. Only the high priest was permitted by God to enter into this Most Holy Place, and he was only allowed in once a year on the Day of Atonement.

According to the Talmud, a book containing sacred Jewish writings, when the high priest went into the Holy of Holies to offer the sacrifice to God, he had to wear a robe with bells along the bottom and a rope tied around his leg. That may sound funny, but there is a reason why he dressed that way, and it is no laughing matter.

The purpose for the noise of the bells was for the people waiting outside. If they heard the bells ringing they knew the priest was still alive and moving. More to the point, the sound of the ringing bells signified that God had received and accepted their sacrifice and offering. How did they know? Because the Presence of Almighty God Himself would come upon the priest so strongly, the priest literally and physically shook in His Presence. It was this shaking that caused the bells on the bottom of the priest's robes to ring. It was the ringing that let the one bringing the sacrifice know that their offering was acceptable to God.

If the offering and sacrifice were not acceptable, God's Presence would not descend upon the priest and the bells on his robes would not ring.

Or, if the priest was unclean or his heart was not right before God, the sacrifice was not accepted and the priest would drop dead!

Since the people outside could not enter into the Holy of Holies without perishing themselves, the rope allowed them to pull the body of the priest from the holy place. This is not a job I would be happy to have, nor was this a time I would like to have lived!

God had a plan for His people, a more intimate plan that was made possible through His Son Jesus.

When Jesus laid down His life for us, He was the final sacrifice, perfect and blameless. His Blood covered the whole world's sin. When He died, the curtain in the temple was torn from the top to the bottom.

It was impossible for any man to have torn this curtain, which was described as being a "hand's breadth" thick. That's 4–6 inches thick of woven fabric! Only the very hand of God, coming down from Heaven, could tear the curtain in two. This is so significant because on the other side of that curtain was where God's Presence previously resided on earth. Jesus' death not only paid for our sins and brought forgiveness and eternal life in Heaven, but the Cross gave us direct access to God; it made a way for the literal Presence of God to reside in each follower of Christ.

Now we don't have to have to go through a high priest, because Jesus Himself became our High Priest. We don't have to rely on anyone else to seek God for us. Now God has prepared a much better way. God wants a personal relationship with each one of His children. He wants to walk with us and talk with us like He did with Adam and Eve in the Garden.

Because of Christ's sacrificial death on the Cross and the shedding of His Blood, when He is our Savior and Lord, we can come to Him just as we are. What a privilege we now have to come into the very Presence of the Most High God!

As we offer our praise and worship to Him, we can enter right into the Holy of Holies with no bells on our clothes and no rope tied to our leg. We can come before Him and lift our prayers before His throne in Heaven! We can walk and talk with our Savior and great High Priest, who made a way for us to approach His throne of grace with confidence (Hebrews 4:16) and have fellowship with Him as friends, both now and forever. Now, instead of bringing the endless blood sacrifices of bulls and goats for "atonement" (Hebrews 13:15), we can come to Christ offering the *"sacrifice of praise"* (Hebrews 13:15). Thank God for the new Covenant!

CHAPTER FOUR

Amazing Grace

*O*ne of the most common lies
Satan uses to attack a new
Believer is through guilt
and condemnation.
But I want to remind you
of something: when Jesus died
on the Cross for you, He did not
pay to redeem half of your sins.
He did not pay for only some
of the world's sins.

GOD WOULD NEVER HAVE ALLOWED His Son Jesus to take on the form of man, go through all the pain and agony of crucifixion, and be separated from His Heavenly Father just to pay for our partial freedom. No way! The Blood of Jesus covers **every** sin, great or small. The Blood of Jesus covers them **ALL**. With His death on the Cross, Jesus paid for all the sins of the world: more than you could commit in ten thousand lifetimes.

Listen to the words of Psalm 103:1-3 *"Bless the LORD, O my soul: and all that is within me, bless his holy name.*

Bless the LORD, O my soul, and forget not all his benefits: Who pardons all your iniquities."

This Scripture passage says that He forgives *ALL* your sins—both the penalty and the shame. Not 10%. Not 50%. Not 75%. *ALL!*

Don't ever allow yourself to wallow in guilt feelings of insecurity or condemnation. These are just attempts by the devil to undermine the death of your Savior and His life within you.

When you feel God's conviction about a sin in your life, confess it, and trust that Jesus has completely washed away both the penalty AND the shame. Don't let the devil lie to you and tell you that the power of your sin's stain is more powerful than the power of Jesus' Blood to forgive your sins and wash you clean.

Satan will try to condemn you by bringing negative thoughts against your mind to damage your faith. Stand firm on the Word! Romans 8:12-13 says, *"Therefore there is now **no condemnation to them which are in Christ**"*

Jesus, who walk not after the flesh, but after the Spirit. For the law of the Spirit of life in Christ Jesus has set you free from the law of sin and death."

Can you see how foolish it is to be trapped in guilt and condemnation? As a Believer you are completely free in Christ! When the Son sets you free, you are free indeed (John 8:36)! Hold fast to God's promise to you.

GOD'S GRACE IS AMAZING!

You cannot live your life in the past or be weighed down by its guilt. It would be a lot harder trying to drive a car while looking in the rear view mirror! Guilt and condemnation are tools of the devil to keep you bound up, depressed, and useless for building up yourself and the Kingdom of God.

None of us is worthy of God's mercy and Jesus' sacrifice on the Cross. We must all learn how to rely on and trust in God's amazing grace. Grace is God's undeserved favor and blessing. By His grace, God has given us something we don't deserve—mercy and forgiveness. We don't have to beg for it. All we have to do is receive God's grace with gratitude and joy—this pleases God's heart.

GOOD NEWS!

The following five verses are often referred to as the "Romans Road," because they are all found in the book of Romans. Together these verses form a clear "road map" of the Gospel of Jesus Christ:

Romans 3:23—"*All have sinned and fall short of the glory of God.*"

Romans 5:8—"*God demonstrates his love for us in this: While we were still sinners Christ died for us.*"

Romans 6:23—"*The wages of sin is death, but the free gift of God is eternal life in Christ Jesus our Lord.*"

Romans 10:9—"*If you confess with your mouth, Jesus as Lord, and believe in your heart that God raised Him from the dead, you will be saved.*"

Romans 10:13—"*Whoever will call on the name of the LORD will be saved.*"

THERE'S ONLY ONE WAY TO HEAVEN!

We are sinners, but God loved us enough to offer us the gift of eternal life by allowing Jesus to die for our sins and offer us the gift of life. All we have to do is confess that we are sinners and believe in Jesus as Savior and Lord!

No one will get to Heaven because he is a good person. ***There is no good deed we can do to earn our salvation.*** Not even keeping the Ten Commandments and following God's law can get us into Heaven. Going to church or Sunday School does not offer us the right to go to Heaven either. Not even believing there is a God will allow us through Heaven's gates of glory. The majority of people who believe there is a Heaven probably think that one of these reasons is going to get them through the gates. Sadly, they are mistaken!

There is only ONE way to Heaven, and it is by God's grace alone, through faith alone, in Jesus Christ alone that we are saved for eternity. *"There is salvation in no one else; for there is no other name under Heaven given among men, by which we must be saved"* (Acts 4:12).

GRACE—A LICENSE TO SIN?

When you were saved, you received God's amazing grace. But just because He has given you His grace doesn't mean you should try to take advantage of His mercy. The book of Jude talks about godless men who exchange the grace of God as a license for immorality, thus denying Jesus Christ as Lord (Jude 1:4). We cannot go around carelessly sinning because we know God will forgive us. The grace of God is by no means a license to sin. Galatians 5:13 reminds us that, *"You were called to freedom, brethren; only do not turn your freedom into an opportunity for the flesh, but through love, serve one another."*

When the Spirit of God comes to live in you, there is a change that takes place inside of you . . . a change you may or may not be able to feel, but a change that people around you will be able to notice.

Paul writes, *"Therefore if any one is in Christ, he is a new creature; the old things passed away; behold, new things have come"* (2 Corinthians 5:17).

In Matthew 7:20, Jesus likened us to fruit trees. Just as we can recognize one tree from another by its fruit and would not try to pick a fruit from thistles, God said that we would recognize His children *"by their fruits."* Your actions will set you apart from others.

Please do not misunderstand me . . . I am **NOT** saying that you can earn your salvation by what you do. Remember: Nothing you *do* can earn your salvation. Your salvation has been completely paid for by the Blood sacrifice of Jesus alone and sealed by your prayer of faith to receive Him as Savior and Lord. You now are motivated to do good things and have a cheerful attitude because of your gratitude and thanks to God for having mercy on you and saving you. Your "good fruit" is an outward expression of the "good work" God has begun in you.

WALKING IN HIS GRACE

Our walk with Christ is a journey of learning to live God's way. Jesus said, *"If anyone would come after Me, he must deny himself and take up his cross daily and follow Me"* (Luke 9:23). You learn to follow Christ by daily laying down the fleshly desires of this world and walking in His grace alone.

There will be times when you fall short and need to ask God to forgive you and then renew your strength to walk in His grace. In these situations where you "miss the mark," do not be overcome with guilt and condemnation. God knows we will sin at times: *"If we say we have no sin, the truth is not in us and we make Him out to be a liar; but if we confess our sins, He is faithful and just to forgive us our sins and cleanse us from all unrighteousness"* (1 John 1:8-9).

Here is God's process for dealing with sin in our lives:

1. The Holy Spirit brings conviction of sin into our lives.

2. We confess our sin to God.

3. We repent of (or "turn away from") the sin.

4. We forget it, and so does He!

Paul said in Philippians 3:13-14: *"But one thing I do: forgetting what lies behind and reaching forward to what lies ahead, I press on toward the goal for the prize of the upward call of God in Christ Jesus."*

Once you have confessed your sins to God and asked Him to forgive you, it's time to move on in the renewed power of the Holy Spirit. This is both a gift from God and your right as a Believer. Psalm 103:12 says that God removes our sins from us *"as far as the east is from the west."*

No matter where you find yourself along the journey of life always remember this:

"By grace you have been saved through faith; and that not of yourselves, it is the gift of God; not as a result of works, so that no one may boast. For we are His workmanship, created in Christ Jesus for good works, which God prepared beforehand so that we would walk in them" (Ephesians 2:8-10).

CHAPTER FIVE

Spiritual Growth

WATER BAPTISM

*O*nce you have decided
to follow Jesus, you now
have an exciting opportunity
to let others know about
your new faith.
Water baptism is
the Scriptural example
that God gave us of how
to publicly declare our
relationship with Jesus.

THERE ARE SEVERAL REASONS WHY BELIEVERS are baptized with water, and the first is obedience. Before Jesus began His public ministry, He declared His total allegiance to God by submitting to water baptism at the hands of a reluctant John the Baptist. In response to John's anxiety over baptizing the Son of God, Jesus said that His baptism was *"fulfilling all righteousness"* (Matthew 3:15). When Jesus was actually immersed in the River Jordan, God responded with an audible voice saying, *"This is My beloved Son, in whom I am well pleased"* (Matthew 3:17). Paul urges us to imitate Christ (1 Corinthians 11:1), and baptism is one of the special ways that we can be Christlike.

Jesus said to His disciples, *"All authority has been given to me in heaven and on earth. Go therefore and make disciples of all the nations, baptizing them in the name of the Father, and the Son, and the Holy Spirit, teaching them to observe all that I commanded you; and lo, I am with you always, even to the end of the age"* (Matthew 28:18-20).

Jesus commanded His disciples to go and teach the world what He had taught them, and He specifically told them to baptize those who believed. So baptism is an act of obedience toward God.

THE SYMBOLISM OF WATER BAPTISM

Baptism is also an outward expression of an inward experience. When you are baptized with water, you are making the statement to all those around you that you are a new creation in Christ, that you love the Lord, and that He is the Lord of your life.

Some people ask, "Do you inherit eternal life by being baptized in water?" The answer is, no. Water baptism is a sign, a symbol, and an outward expression of an inward change. And it's something Scripture instructs us to do.

Think about it this way. When people get married they exchange wedding rings. The wedding ring is an outward sign or symbol that the person is married.

Does the wearing of a wedding ring make you married? No. On the other hand, are you suddenly not married because you don't wear your wedding ring? Of course not! The wedding ring is a symbol of something that has taken place in your life.

It's the same with water baptism. As you go under the water, it's as though you're laying down your old life. You are, in a sense, dying as Christ died on the Cross for your sins. Then you rise up, washed and cleansed, resurrected to a new life just like Jesus. You are a new person by the faith you have in God. Colossians 2:12 says that we have "been **buried with Him (Jesus) in baptism** in which you were also raised up with Him through faith in the working of God, who raised Him from the dead." The act of water baptism is a symbol of your repentant heart and your conversion into Christianity.

In the book of Acts, the Apostle Peter was preaching to a large crowd. When the people were moved by his words and asked how they should respond, Peter replied, "Repent, and each of you be baptized, everyone of you, in *the name of Jesus Christ for the forgiveness of your sins; and you will receive the gift of the Holy Spirit."* In verse 41 we read that those who accepted the message of salvation were baptized, and about 3,000 were added to the early Church that day! (Acts 2:38-41)

If you were to continue reading throughout the book of Acts, you would see that as people accepted the message of Jesus Christ, they were baptized with water as an outward demonstration of their new faith.

So water baptism is significant because Jesus wants us to publicly declare our love for Him. Water baptism is an expression of a repentant heart and a symbol of your conversion into the Christian faith.

THE TRINITY

I'm interjecting a very short explanation of the Trinity here, because I feel it will be helpful to you as we talk about being filled with the Holy Spirit. Also, as you become more established in your faith, it's important for you to understand some foundational truths about the Trinity—God the Father, God the Son, and God the Holy Spirit.

The concept of the Trinity is a mystery. And yes, it's difficult to comprehend or explain the unity of three separate, distinct persons in one God. In the Trinity, we have God the Father, Who is exalted far above us in Heaven; Jesus Christ the Son, Who saves us, and the Holy Spirit, Who comes to live in us as well.

THE HOLY SPIRIT

God the Father and God the Son often receive the most attention when people talk about the Trinity. But the Holy Spirit is a vital part of the Trinity we should not neglect.

The Bible says that the Holy Spirit is our Teacher who *"guides us into all truth"* (John 16:13). He is our Comforter and our Teacher (John 14:26). The Spirit of God is also described as a down payment for your life. Second Corinthians 5:5 declares, *"Now it is God who has made us for this very purpose and has given us the Spirit as a deposit, guaranteeing what is to come."*

To understand the Holy Spirit, it's best to study the book of Acts. Throughout this book, you will see the roles that He plays in the lives of Believers. When the Holy Spirit is mentioned, many times He is giving instruction and guidance to the disciples. Some examples are found in Acts 1:2 and 10:9-22.

The Holy Spirit also strengthens and encourages the Church. For example, in Acts 9:31 we read, *"So the church throughout Judea and Galilee and Samaria enjoyed peace, being built up; and going on in the fear of the Lord and in the comfort of the Holy Spirit, it continued to increase."* This verse is so significant because it shows how the Holy Spirit helped people after the outpouring of His Presence as recorded in Acts 2.

In fact, the Holy Spirit had never resided within people until Jesus returned to His Father in Heaven (Acts 1). You see, in the Old Testament, the Holy Spirit *came upon* people for a brief period of time and a specific purpose only. Examples of this are found in the book of Judges, where on four separate occasions, Scripture comments that the *"Spirit of God came upon him (Sampson) might-ily"* (Judges 14:6, 19; 15:14). This occurred when the Holy Spirit worked through Sampson with incredible strength and power to accomplish a task.

This pattern continues throughout the Old Testament.

THE GIFT OF THE HOLY SPIRIT

All of this changed when Jesus left earth to return to Heaven. Jesus tells His disciples to go and wait for the promise of His Father: *"He commanded them not to leave Jerusalem, but to wait for what the Father had promised, which, He said, 'you heard of from me'"* (Acts 1:4). What was this promise that Jesus had spoke of? He gives the answer in verse 5: *"For John baptized with water, but you will be baptized with the Holy Spirit."* This gift of His Father is the blessed Holy Spirit!

The incredible news is that now the Holy Spirit is not coming for a specific moment and purpose. He is coming to fill all Believers everywhere and at all times!

In Acts 1:8, Jesus said that two things would happen after they received the Holy Spirit:

1. *"He will give you power"*
2. *"You will be my witnesses"*

This word "witnesses" means to "give evidence to" or "testify." The Holy Spirit's power would enable people to give evidence that Jesus is Who He claims to be. And this is exactly what happened!

EMPOWERED!

The disciples did just what Jesus told them to do; they went to Jerusalem and waited in an upper room. As they waited, they began to praise God and the Promise came. The disciples were filled with the Holy Spirit! The Holy Spirit then gave them boldness to preach and testify of God's greatness, and when they did, miracles followed.

Paul even told people that he was not going to use eloquent speech or enticing words of wisdom to persuade them, but that he would come in a *"demonstration of the Spirit and the power."* In that way, the people's faith would not rest on man's wisdom but in God's power (1 Corinthians 2:4-5).

The Holy Spirit empowered and enabled the early Church to practically evangelize the entire world without having a Bible or any of the modern technology we have today like printing presses, radio, television, or the Internet. History records that the entire known world was reached with the Gospel within the first 200 years after the death and resurrection of Christ.

Everywhere the early Christians went, they shared the Gospel; it just flowed out of them as a result of their being filled with the Holy Spirit.

EVEN GREATER WORKS!

The very shadow of the Apostle Peter brought healing to the sick (Acts 5:15). This was not because of Peter himself, but happened because Peter was filled with the Holy Spirit of God.

Jesus said that His followers will do even *"greater things"* than He did when He walked on the earth (John 14:12). How? Because He was going to His Father in Heaven and would send the "Comforter," the Holy Spirit.

The same Holy Spirit who filled, empowered, and equipped Jesus at His baptism in the Jordan River would now fill *US*, empowering and equiping *us* to do the work of the ministry (Acts 1: 4-5, 8; John 14:12). Jesus healed the sick, He opened the eyes of the blind, the crippled walked, lives were restored, and even the dead were raised back to life! With all of these miracles, Jesus said that we would do even *greater works.* We are able to do these things only through the empowering Spirit of God, and He intends for us to access His power. He has delegated His power and authority to *US.*

In Acts 3, Peter said to a lame man, *"I do not possess silver and gold, but what I do have I give to you: In the name of Jesus Christ the Nazarene—walk!"* What did Peter have? Power! Where did he get it? The Holy Spirit.

At least twice Jesus said, *"As the Father has sent Me, I also send you"* (John 17:18, John 20:21). How did the Father send Jesus? With all power and all authority. Jesus says in Matthew 28:18, *"All authority has been given to Me in heaven and on earth."*

ALL AUTHORITY!

Since Jesus was sent here by His Father with ALL authority, and He sends us as His Father sent Him, then we have been delegated the same power as was delegated to Christ! 1 John 4:17 says, *"As He is, so also are we in this world."* Wow!

Would God intend for only the first century Church to walk in His power? No, certainly not! These gifts the disciples and the early Church experienced did not die out thousands of years ago contrary to what many "theologians" preach today. Jesus is the same yesterday, today, and forever (Hebrews 13:8.) God intends for us to walk in this same power today that Jesus did when He lived here on earth.

BAPTISM OF THE HOLY SPIRIT

You may wonder how it could be possible for us as Believers to do the same miracles Jesus did while on earth. How could Jesus say that we would do even *greater* things than He did? The answer is found in the person of the Holy Spirit.

We have talked about water baptism, but there is a second baptism I want to share with you: the baptism of the Holy Spirit.

In Acts 2:38-39 the Apostle Peter said, *"Repent, and each of you be baptized in the name of Jesus Christ for the forgiveness of your sins; and you will receive the gift of the Holy Spirit. For the promise is for you and your children and for all who are far off, as many as the Lord our God will call to Himself."*

Notice the three points Peter makes here:

1. Repent. To "repent" means to turn **away from**

your selfish desires and your sinful ways and **turn toward** the Kingdom of God and His ways.

2. Be baptized. Peter was speaking about water baptism here.
3. Receive the gift of the Holy Spirit.

Some churches and denominations today teach that when you become born again, you receive Jesus and, by receiving Jesus, you receive the Holy Spirit.

Other churches and denominations teach that the empowering and infilling of the Holy Spirit was given only to the disciples or the Believers in the days of Christ, or in the early Church.

Still others believe that *salvation* and being *filled with the Holy Spirit* are indeed two separate experiences. And, that this gift—this promise of the Holy Spirit—is available to all Believers today.

Regardless of differing church traditions, there are rules of interpretation and there are exceptions to the rules. Jesus said in Matthew 18:16, "*In the mouth of two or three witnesses every word should be established.*" Even in most judicial systems, to convict a person of a capital crime requires the eyewitness testimony of at least two people. Otherwise, it's just one person's word against another's. The good news is that there are many witnesses to the Holy Spirit in Scripture.

The New Testament refers to the experience of Believers receiving the Holy Spirit in several ways. Sometimes, it is referred to as a *"gift"* (Acts 2:38). Other times Scripture says, *"poured out"* (Acts 10:45). Sometimes the reference is to being *"filled"* (Acts 2:4). *"Baptized with"* the Holy Ghost or Holy Spirit is yet another reference (Mark 1:8; Acts 1:5). As you study these Scriptures, you will discover that these various references are interchangeable in meaning.

I believe the Bibles clearly teaches that salvation and the baptism with the Holy Spirit are two separate, unique experiences.

Here's one reference to that: When the Apostles in Jerusalem heard that Samaria had accepted the Word of God, they sent Peter and John to Believers there.

Why? Peter and John were sent to Samaria for a purpose! The Apostles in Jerusalem had heard that Samaria had accepted the Word of God. Why send Peter and John? Because they had also heard that the Believers in Samaria had not yet received the Holy Spirit.

Acts 8: 14–17 says, *"When Peter and John arrived, they prayed for these Christians to receive the Holy Spirit,* **because the Holy Spirit had not yet come upon any of them;** *they had simply been baptized into the name of the Lord Jesus. Then Peter and John placed their hands on the Believers, and they received the Holy Spirit."*

So here we find people who had believed. They were referred to as Christians. They had been baptized in water. But for some reason, the Apostles in Jerusalem felt these newly born-again Christians lacked something important. They sent Peter and John to lay hands on them to receive the Holy Spirit.

Here's another reference to salvation and the baptism

of the Holy Spirit being two distinct experiences:

In Acts 19, Paul came through the city of Corinth where many had become followers of Jesus Christ. What does "followers of Jesus Christ" mean? Surely, it means that these people had repented. They had accepted or invited Jesus Christ into their lives. They believed Him to be the resurrected Son of the living God, and they had been baptized with water.

Paul asked them, *"Did you receive the Holy Spirit when you believed?"* Why would he ask this question if believing on Jesus as Lord and the baptism of the Holy Spirit were one and the same experience?

They said to Paul, *"No, we have not even heard whether there is a Holy Spirit"* (verse 2). Clearly, they were Believers. Clearly, they were called disciples (verse 1). Then Paul *"laid his hands upon them."* When he did, *"the Holy Spirit came on them, and they began speaking with tongues and prophesying"* (verse 6).

In both these examples, we see the pattern which Peter refers to in Acts 2:38; believe, be baptized, and receive the Holy Spirit. However, let's not be too quick to make a "rule" out of this pattern.

In Acts 9 we read about the conversion of Saul. Saul was a devout Jew who persecuted the Church and Christians. On the road to Damascus, Jesus appeared to him and asked, *"Why do your persecute Me?"* In this experience, Saul was both blinded physically and converted spiritually. Days later a man named Ananias came and put his hands on Saul and prayed that he would receive his sight and be filled with the Holy Spirit. Saul immediately received his sight, was filled with the Holy Spirit, and *then* was baptized. Saul was renamed Paul and went on to become one of the greatest of all the Apostles, writing almost two-thirds of the entire New Testament.

We could point to various examples in Scripture where the sequence differs regarding: 1) repentance, 2) water baptism and 3) receiving the Holy Spirit.

Is it possible to be baptized before you repent? Yes, but it would be no more effective than a person taking a bath. Why? Because the act of repentance and asking Jesus to be the Lord of your life is a prerequisite to being baptized in water or filled with the Spirit.

But clearly we have seen that it is possible to repent and then be filled with the Holy Spirit before a person is baptized in water, just as we have seen that it's possible to repent, then be baptized in water, and then be baptized in the Holy Spirit.

THE EXAMPLE OF JESUS

While Jesus Christ was here on earth, the disciples saw in Him the physical form of God the Son. Jesus Christ is the living Son of God made flesh on earth.

The Bible says, "*And the Word became flesh, and dwelt among us, and we saw His glory, glory as of the only begotten from the Father, full of grace and truth*" (John 1:14).

Again, Philippians 2:6–7 tells us, "*Who (Jesus), being in the form of God, thought it not robbery to be equal with*

God: But made himself of no reputation, and took upon him the form of a servant, and was made in the likeness of men."

God, in the person of the Son, stepped out of Heaven, came to this earth, took upon Himself the form of flesh and blood, lived a sinless life, was crucified, buried and resurrected on the third day. Afterwards, He walked the earth for many days showing infallible proofs of His resurrection to hundreds of people. Soon afterward, He ascended back to Heaven where He now sits at the right hand of God.

When Jesus Christ came to this earth, He came in the form of a baby. He didn't just show up one day as a full-grown man claiming to be the Son of God. The Holy Spirit conceived Jesus in the Virgin Mary. In Luke 1:35 we read, *"The Holy Ghost shall come upon thee, and the power of the Highest shall overshadow thee: therefore also that holy thing which shall be born of thee shall be called the Son of God."* Nine months later, just as the gestation period is with any baby, Jesus was born.

There is a parallel here to our new birth experience. The same Holy Spirit, Who impregnated the Virgin Mary with the seed of Jesus, now takes the spiritual seed of Christ and impregnates us. Christ was born in you. No, it didn't take a nine-month gestation period for that to happen. It happened the moment you invited Him into your life and asked Him to forgive your sins and make you God's child.

The Apostle Paul called it the mystery of the Gospel: *"Christ in you, the hope of glory"* (Colossians 1:27). When the Holy Spirit places the spiritual seed of Christ within us, we are born again. This means Christ is born in us.

This is exactly what Jesus referred to when He was speaking to Nicodemus and said, *"You must be born again"* (John 3:13). In our salvation experience, it's the Holy Spirit who comes and places within us the seed of Christ.

Later in Jesus' ministry He would say, *"If you have seen me, you have seen the Father."* What Jesus was referring to was similar to the old adages "like father like son." Jesus even said that He only spoke the things His Father spoke (John 8:28).

While Jesus was on earth, He was all God, but He was the person of God the Son. Colossians 2:9 says, *"For in him dwelleth all the fullness of the Godhead bodily."* That means the fullness of the Father and the fullness of the Son and the fullness of the Holy Spirit lived in Jesus.

Even though Jesus could say, *"If you have seen me you have seen the Father,"* He was not God the Father while on earth. Nor was He God the Holy Spirit. However, God the Holy Spirit came to earth and filled and empowered the life of Christ.

EMPOWERED FOR MINISTRY

When Jesus was baptized with water in the Jordan River by John the Baptist, the Heavens opened and the Holy Spirit descended in a bodily form like a dove upon Him, and the voice of God spoke, *"This is my son in whom I am well pleased"* (Luke 3:22). The third person of the Trinity, the blessed Holy Spirit, had come to live in Jesus to empower His life.

John the Baptist said in John 1:33-34, *"I did not recognize Him (Jesus), but He (the Father) who sent me to baptize in water said to me, 'He upon whom you see the Spirit descending and remaining upon Him* (abiding, continuing, dwelling), *this is the One who baptizes* (will baptize you, immerse, submerge you) *in the Holy Spirit.' I myself have seen, and have testified that this is the Son of God."*

It was only *after* this experience of the indwelling of the Holy Spirit that Jesus began His ministry (Matthew 3:11-17; 4:17).

You may be asking, "David, do you mean to tell me that Jesus needed the empowerment of the Holy Spirit to work the works of God?" Yes, I do!

Yes, Jesus was the Son of God, but it was the Holy Spirit Who empowered Jesus' life and ministry.

Jesus knew that one day He would be crucified. One day He would be resurrected. One day He would ascend to His Father in Heaven. And, one day He would commission us, the Church, to go into all the world and preach the Gospel to every person.

How could we possibly do that without the same power that Jesus possessed? That's why Jesus said, *"As my Father sent me even so send I you."* That's why Jesus told the disciples that He was going to His Father in Heaven, but that they were to wait in Jerusalem until they were filled with the same power that filled Him.

Jesus Himself needed to be filled with the Holy Spirit to work the works of His Heavenly Father. The disciples needed the experience of being filled with the Holy Spirit to work the works of God. And we need the experience of being filled with the Holy Spirit to work the works of God!

The same Holy Spirit Who filled Jesus as He was baptized before He began His ministry also filled the disciples in the upper room. At that point, their ministry began. Jesus said to His disciples in Acts 1:8, *"You will receive power when the Holy Ghost is come upon you and you will be witnesses to me both in Jerusalem and in all Judea, and in Samaria, and to the farthermost parts of the earth."*

The good news is that the same Holy Spirit comes to fill the Church today! The Holy Spirit is a gift from God. He is for all Believers, and I believe God intends for His whole Church to be filled with the power of the Holy Spirit.

Jesus is seated at the right hand of His Father in Heaven and eagerly waits to pour out His Spirit upon those who obey.

God did not give birth to an anemic Church. God intended for His Church to be filled with His Spirit and His power. The Bible says that God gives His Spirit to us without limits (John 3:34)! God wants His power to be operating in your life. This is His gift to you, and it is your destiny to be His witness.

I believe that the Scriptures teach and encourage us to pursue the Baptism of the Holy Spirit, Who gives us the power to live victoriously for Christ and work the works of God.

John the Baptist said, *"I baptize you with water for repentance, but after me will come one who is more powerful than I, whose sandals I am not fit to carry.* **He will baptize you with the Holy Spirit and with fire"** (Matthew 3:11-17).

When we receive the indwelling presence of the Holy Spirit, Jesus is the one Who baptizes us in the Holy Spirit. Remember John the Baptist's words in John 1:33? *"This is the One (Jesus) who baptizes in the Holy Spirit."*

SOME IMPORTANT ATTRIBUTES OF GOD

Jesus, God the Son was *born* of the Holy Spirit. Later, when He was baptized by John, He was *filled* with the Holy Spirit.

The Scripture says, *"In Him dwelled the fullness of the Godhead bodily"* (Colossians 2:9). Jesus said, *"If you have seen Me, you have seen the Father, for I and the Father are One"* (John 10:30). Jesus clearly reflected the heart and the character of the Father. His behavior and speech reflected the Father, and His essence was also fully God. In fact, one of Jesus' names is Emmanuel, which literally means "God with us."

While Jesus said that He only spoke and did what the Father desired, He also had a distinct personality. This is one of the great "mysteries of the faith." Jesus is both the Son of God *and* God the Son.

When we invite Jesus Christ into our hearts and become born again, the personality, nature, and attributes of Christ are born in us. They are placed there by the Holy Spirit, just as the Holy Spirit placed the spiritual seed of Christ in the Virgin Mary.

In the Old Testament, the Holy Spirit did appear, but

He came *upon* people for a specific task and purpose. In those days, the Spirit of God did not *live* in men. As the Spirit of God came upon men, He often gave extraordinary strength in battle to men like David and Samson and supernatural insights to prophets like Isaiah, Ezekiel and Daniel. In fact, the writers of all the books of the Bible, including the Old Testament, wrote the sacred Scriptures, as they were led by the Holy Spirit.

However, beginning with Jesus, the Holy Spirit comes to abide, dwell, and continue to be present with us. With the return of Jesus to Heaven came the "permanent" ministry of the Holy Spirit. Speaking to His disciples in Acts 1:5, Jesus said, *"For John truly baptized with water; but ye shall be baptized with the Holy Ghost not many days hence."*

He went on to say in Acts 1:8 that the Holy Spirit is going to come upon His disciples and literally take up residence with them. As a Believer, your body is now the *"temple of the Holy Spirit"* (1 Corinthians 3:16).

The Holy Spirit lives within us. He is our Guide and our Counselor. He leads us into all Truth. He interprets Scripture for us, and He empowers us, just as He empowered Jesus for His earthly ministry. Jesus is our example for the Christian life. He was filled, empowered, and equipped by the Holy Spirit, as we must be.

GOD'S TRUTH

Today, there are many people in the Church with a weak

and anemic faith. They may have repented. They may even have been baptized in water. But, despite the precious promise of God, they are not filled with the Person and the empowerment of the Holy Spirit.

The last thing I want to do is confuse you. My purpose in bringing up these different positions is to inform you. In your Christian walk you will come across people who hold fast to one of these differing viewpoints.

Volumes of books have been written on the subject of the Holy Spirit. It's not my intention in this book to try to familiarize you with all the different doctrinal beliefs of various churches about the Holy Spirit.

I am not a theologian. I am simply a student of the Bible. Throughout this book, I am sharing with you what the Bible says, not what a church says and not what a particular denomination says.

Don't be anxious about the various perspectives; you simply need to know that people differ on their various interpretations of Scripture. I remember a preacher once saying he knew that not everyone in his denomination believed the same way. He went on to say he understood not even everyone in the church he pastored interpreted Scripture the same. Then he finally said, "Even my wife and I don't agree on every point of Scripture."

As you read this book, I'm asking you to pray and ask God to speak to you and reveal His truth to your heart. What I have to say is not as important as what God has to say to you.

TAKE HOLD OF THE PROMISE!

We're living in what could be the last days of human history. We may very well be the generation who ushers in the Second Coming of Christ. If this is true, then now, more than ever, we must listen to the teachings in the book of Acts. The Church must use wisdom and take advice from these first disciples. We must stand up with boldness and walk in the victory that is already ours!

We must reach out and take hold of the Father's promise: the blessed Holy Spirit to equip and empower us to do His will! God said that in the last days He would pour out His Spirit on all people (Acts 2:17-18). Today God is looking for those who are hungry for Him. He is seeking those who are willing to obey Him with boldness.

Get ready to see demonstrations of God's power like never seen before on earth. God is sweeping across this earth and pouring out His Spirit on disciples this very moment. I know that you and I are not going to be passed by. It's time to walk in the power in which God intends for His Church: 100% victory, over 100% of the enemy's power, 100% of the time!

According to Matthew 28, we are commanded to make disciples of all nations, baptizing them in the name of the Father, the Son, and the Holy Spirit. This is our commission; this is our duty. It's time for the Church to take hold of this promise. And, now that you are a Believer, this includes YOU! Even if you are a new Christian, you're a part of the priestly ministry of Christ.

Peter writes, *"You are a chosen generation, a royal priesthood, a holy nation, His own special people, that you may proclaim the praises of Him who called you out of darkness into His light"* (1 Peter 2:9). As inconceivable as it may sound to you, every Believer is a "holy priest" to God, having received God-given authority to represent the Lord in the world by the power of His Holy Spirit.

BE FILLED WITH THE HOLY SPIRIT!

Please do not quickly pass over this section of the book. In the world in which we're living today, the power of God is the vital ingredient you need operating in your life. The Church has the ability to do the miracles that Jesus and the early disciples did. So why aren't we?

Perhaps apathy is looming over our world. Too many Christians today feel like there is nothing they can possibly do to make a difference in this world. Perhaps it's because some have been saved but not filled, equipped, and empowered with the Holy Spirit.

It's time for the Church, the Body of Christ, to stand up and take the spiritual offensive to reach our families, communities, school systems, work places, cities, and the nations of this world with the saving grace and the power of the living God! With the enabling of the Holy Spirit, you **CAN** make a difference! The time is **NOW!** If you have not already been filled with the Holy Spirit, I invite you to allow Jesus to fill you with His Holy Spirit and power. Pray this prayer with me right now:

Dear Heavenly Father, You promise in the Bible to send Your disciples the gift of the Holy Spirit. Lord, I want more of You in my life. I need more of Your power, so please send your Holy Spirit to fill me right now. Jesus, cleanse my heart and baptize me with Your precious Holy Spirit. Thank You for this amazing gift! Please give me the passion to serve You and do what You did while You were here on earth. Please fill me with the Holy Spirit's power to tell others about Your great love. Holy Spirit, You are welcome in my life. I open my heart to You. In Jesus' name I pray, Amen.

Now receive God's Holy Spirit into your heart and live in all the fullness of His power.

SECTION TWO

ABIDING *in* JESUS

CHAPTER SIX

Read God's Word

*Y*ou have a physical body
that you feed every day.
In the same way,
you have a spirit
that needs to be fed
healthy spiritual food
on a daily basis.

THINK ABOUT IT THIS WAY. How long could you go without eating? A day? No problem. But how would you feel at the end of that day?

How about a week? This is more challenging, but you could probably do that. Then again, how would you feel at the end of that week? Tired? Most likely. Weak? Certainly. How about going without food for 30 days–40 days . . . how long would it take before your body gave out completely and you died?

God established this "Principle of Self-Preservation" to keep us alive and healthy: we must eat to live. You don't need to believe in this principle if you don't want to; just violate it see what happens. After 30 days . . . 40 days . . . perhaps even 50 days . . . you will die.

The same principle holds true spiritually. What is our spiritual nourishment? The Word of God. The longer we go without the life it contains, the weaker our spirits become. The life of Christ within your spirit must be fed in order to grow strong and stay healthy. Reading the Bible is nourishment to your spirit. Praising Him with worship and spiritual songs is like drinking from the River of Life (Revelation 22:1).

Spending time talking with Him is an essential ingredient in developing a strong and meaningful relationship with Christ. As you read Scripture, soon you will find that, although written thousands of years ago, its words are still so very relevant to your life today. Within its pages you will find stories of people with whom you can identify, new lessons to learn, refreshment for your soul, and comfort in your times of need.

DAILY DEVOTIONS

Jesus prayed, "*Give us this day our **daily** bread*" (Matthew 6:11). It's so important for you to find time every day when you can read the Word of God and eat "spiritual bread." Christians often refer to this time as "having devotions."

Devotions are simply a quiet time of the day devoted to talking with God, worshipping Him, and learning what His Holy Spirit has to teach you. God will speak to you through His Word, and you will find that it gives you strength for your day.

This quiet time can be in the morning or in the evening. The time is not important; what *is* important is the *quality* of time you spend.

You are not made more holy than other Believers because you spend more time in the Word than they do. Your quiet time with God should be motivated out of love for Him rather than by the clock.

SPENDING TIME WITH GOD

When you love someone and they are special to you, it's only natural that you want to spend time with that person. This is how it is in the time you spend with the Lord. Your time with Him is a good discipline, but it should not be a ritual. If you missed reading God's Word one day, don't feel guilty. Many Christians are so bound up with the routine of devotions that the purpose of having a quiet, quality time with the Lord is lost. This is not what God wants at all!

God understands that your life is busy with deadlines to meet and bills to pay. What He asks is that you dedicate time to be with Him as a part of your day and that you learn to make Him a living Presence throughout your day. Paul said we should "*Pray without ceasing*" (1 Thessalonians 5:17). In essence, this means that the Lord should be our holy "preoccupation," regardless of what we're doing. Jesus said, "*Abide in me and I will abide in you*" (John 15:4). Jesus is challenging us to "stay connected" to Him at all times, in all of our thoughts and actions, so that we can be fruitful in our service to Him.

God gave His only Son as a sacrifice so that you could have everlasting life in Heaven with Him. He loves you so much and longs to spend time with you. His desire is to have a relationship with you. This relationship thrives and grows as you spend time fellowshipping with Him and reading His Word.

There is no doubt in my mind that your devotions will become a special time for you, a time when you feel the very Presence of God next to you, a time that you will long for daily, and a state of mind that you will carry with you throughout your day. Spending time with God in His Word is one of the practical ways to develop your relationship with Him.

HEARING GOD'S VOICE

Remember that Christianity is a *relationship* with a living God. You cannot have a relationship with someone without speaking to them. There are several ways to communicate with God. And, yes, God **will** speak back to you. You don't have to expect a bolt of lighting from the sky or a deep voice booming out of the clouds. God speaks to His children in many different ways.

One of the ways that God speaks is through His Word. This is another reason why your devotion times are so important; they are opportunities for God to speak to you. He will reveal truth, wisdom, insights, and practical help relevant to your life if you will open your heart to receive what He has to say.

Another way that God speaks is with a *"still small voice"* (1 Kings 19:12). His voice usually isn't audible, although it could be. More often, it's a peace you feel in your heart, a confidence, a "knowing" that your Lord is speaking to you.

An awareness of God's peace in our hearts is often the way that He speaks to us and directs our lives. Philippians 4:7 says, *"The peace of God, which passes all understanding, will keep your hearts and minds through Christ Jesus."* As Christians, we are to *"let the peace of God guard our hearts"* (Colossians 3:15).

However God speaks to you, His voice is always consistent with the Holy Spirit and the Holy Scriptures.

'MY SHEEP KNOW MY VOICE'

One way that Jesus is referred to in the Bible is as a Shepherd, and we are called His sheep. You may know the familiar words of the 23ᴿᴰ Psalm: *"The Lord is my shepherd."*

In the book of John, Jesus said, *"The man who enters by the gate is the shepherd of his sheep. The watchman opens the gate for him, and the sheep listen to His voice. He calls his own sheep by name and leads them out. When he has brought out all his own, he goes ahead of them, and his sheep follow him because they know his voice. But they will never follow a stranger; in fact, they will run away from him because they do not recognize a stranger's voice"* (John 10:2-5).

The more time you spend with the Lord, the more familiar you will become with His voice. Just as you recognize the voice of a friend on the other end of the telephone, when you spend time getting to know the Lord, it will be easier for you to recognize when He's speaking to you. You will know your Shepherd's voice, and you will follow Him; you won't follow a stranger's voice.

If you ever have doubt or confusion in your heart about hearing God's voice, talk about this with God in prayer. Satan would love for you to think God is not speaking to you and that the voice you hear in your head is simply your own imagination. Do not be overcome by the lies of the devil.

If you are confused, ask the Lord to help you. 1 Corinthians 14:33 says, *"God is not a God of confusion but (a God) of peace."* He will give you peace and confirm His answer to you if you ask Him. You always can check what you believe you are hearing against the Bible: God *always* acts in agreement with His written Word and never contradicts His own Scripture.

YOU HAVE A DIRECT LINE TO GOD!

God can also speak to you through other people.

However, you must remember that "*no prophecy of Scripture is of any private interpretation*" (2 Peter 1:20). In other words, when God uses a person to speak His will, a true prophetic word must line up with Scripture and confirm what the Lord has already spoken to you. It's important to make sure that the counsel that you receive in your life comes from people who trust Christ and who walk by the Spirit of God.

As a new Believer, it's a sad but important thing for you to know that some Christians try to control people by acting as though they are the voice of God for others. Only God's Spirit within you will be able to tell if someone is truly communicating God's heart to you or not. Beware of the attempts of other people to manipulate you. And remember, people can be sincerely wrong. Godly counsel will be rooted in God's Word and come with His peace.

If God has not already spoken to your spirit about what someone else is saying to you, then you can probably assume that the message is not from God. We need to have a teachable heart and allow Spirit-led people to speak God's truths into our lives. But we're not required to embrace every notion or impulse from others about our lives. If you don't sense in your spirit that someone else's word lines up with God's Word, hit the "eject button."

God has a direct line to you and you have a direct line to God! While He may use another Christian to *confirm* something in our lives and to be a source of encouragement and care, God does not use people to *direct* our lives. God Himself directs our lives. He does so through His Word, through that "still small voice" in our hearts, and sometimes as a confirmation through another person.

The Bible says, *"Beloved, do not believe every spirit, but test the spirits to see whether they are from God, because many false prophets have gone out into the world"* (1 John 4:1). At first glance, you may think it is easy to tell an evil spirit from something holy. But be cautious. The Bible warns us, *"Satan himself masquerades as an angel of light. It is not surprising then, if his servants masquerade as servants of righteousness"* (2 Corinthians 11:14-15).

The better you know God, the quicker you will be able to recognize an imposter. The devil is a deceptive and devious master of lies; you must stay on your spiritual toes and always *test* the spirits in prayer to make sure they are truly from God. This is one reason it's so important to stay close to the Lord in your daily devotional times. By spending time talking to Him, listening to Him, worshipping Him, and reading His Word, you will learn to recognize His voice. In this way, you will be protected from deception in whatever form it may come!

CHAPTER SEVEN

Worship and Pray

*I*n this chapter, I want to spend
a little more time sharing
with you about the importance
of coming into God's Presence
during your devotional time
to worship Him and talk
with Him. Worship and prayer
are so important for Christians: only
in His Presence are we changed, and
so many things become possible in
God's Presence!

BY SPENDING TIME WITH HIM, you will be transformed . . . changed . . . into the image of His Son, Jesus Christ. This is God's goal for you—to make you more and more like Jesus with each passing day.

Worship and prayer will help you to surrender your fears, frustrations, hurts, and problems to the Lord. Worship and prayer are your recognition that He **alone** holds the answers to your struggles and that you cannot resolve your problems in your own strength.

If you truly want to know God; if you want Him to change and transform you; if you hunger for an intimate relationship with Him; if you recognize that you need His power and strength to help you bring wholeness and healing to yourself and others . . . then spend time with God in His Presence, worshipping Him and talking with Him.

WHAT IS WORSHIP?

God has placed within every human being a hunger to worship. God wants to satisfy that hunger as we direct our devotion and adoration toward Him—the one true God.

Worship is expressed in countless ways in many different church traditions and cultures. Yet, true God-honoring, Christ-centered, Spirit-led worship always involves expressions of gratitude, awe, and devotion. Simply put, worship is a marriage of two words—"worth" and "ship." When we worship with sincerity, we are literally expressing back to God His enormous "worth" or value in our lives.

WHY WORSHIP?

God does not want you to worship Him because He needs your worship. He wants you to worship Him because *YOU* need that kind of intimate connection for YOURSELF, and because He is completely worthy of your devotion!

When you worship the Lord, you acknowledge that there is a Higher Being Who is greater than you. You acknowledge that there IS a living God and that He is Lord over your life. This will cause you to draw upon His strength for victory in every situation you face.

Worship will lift you up and out of the troubles of this world and set you in the realm of His Spirit. There the Lord can shower you with His Presence and confirm that ***HE IS IN CONTROL*** of all things!

There is an old hymn that says, "Oh what fellowship, oh what joy divine, leaning on the everlasting arms." True worship brings us to that peaceful place where we exchange our worries for the incredible joy of intimate friendship with the Living God.

HOW DO I WORSHIP GOD?

Worshipping God and praising Him are typically thought of in reference to music. Yet there are actually many ways to express genuine worship to God.

The Bible says, "*Shout to the Lord, all the earth, burst into jubilant song with music; make music to the Lord with the harp and the sound of singing, with trumpets and the blast of the ram's horn, shout for joy before the Lord, the King"* (Psalm 98: 4-6). Making music with instruments, singing, and shouts of joy are all expressions of praise to God. If you are a musician, then worship the Lord with your instrument. He has given you the talent and ability, and when you play for Him, you are giving Him glory and worship. As you do this, both God and you will be blessed.

One of the best "instruments" I can play is my own two hands. *"Clap your hands, all you nations; shout to God with cries of joy"* (Psalm 47:1). Handclapping is a form of praise.

You can also lift your hands toward Heaven in a sign of worship to the Lord. *"Lift up your hands in the sanctuary and praise the Lord"* (Psalm 147:2). David said in Psalms 63:4, *"I will lift up my hands in Your name."*

The Bible is filled with verses telling us that singing is a form of worship. This one verse alone tells us to sing four times: *"Sing praises to God, sing praises; sing praises to our King, sing praises"* (Psalm 47:6). You do not have to be an expert vocalist to sing to the Lord. God hears you singing from your heart, not your vocal cords!

Shouts of joy are also worship. There are more than 30 references in the Bible to the people of God **shouting**. Psalm 5:11 says, *"Let all those that put their trust in thee rejoice; let them ever shout for joy, because thou defendest them: let them also that love thy name be joyful in thee."* Psalm 32:11 says, *"Rejoice in the Lord and be glad, you righteous; sing, all you who are upright in heart!"* Psalm

47:1 says, "*O clap your hands, all you people; shout unto God with the voice of triumph.*"

Although shouting to God may sound odd, think of it this way: if you were at a sporting event and your team just took the field, what do you usually do? You shout! If the team you were rooting for scored, or better yet, won the game, would you be excited? Can you see yourself shouting for victory? The whole stadium would be filled with loud clapping and shouting! Well, God has fought and won a mighty battle for YOU! It is perfectly understandable why a Christian would want to shout with excitement, joy, and victory to God!

Some people dance before the Lord as they worship Him. The Bible says that the Spirit of the Lord came upon King David and, "*David danced before the Lord with all his might*" (2 Samuel 6:14).

GIVING IS A FORM OF WORSHIP

A special way to worship God is through the privilege of giving monetary gifts to Him. These gifts are often referred to as "tithes," which simply means giving God back 10% of what *He* has given *YOU*.

The Bible teaches about tithing in Malachi 3:8-12:

"*Will a man rob God? Yet you are robbing Me! But you say, 'How have we robbed you?' In tithes and offerings. You are cursed with a curse, for you are robbing me, the whole nation of you! Bring the whole tithe into the storehouse, that there may be food in my house. Test me in this' says the*

Lord Almighty, 'and see if I will not throw open the flood-gates of Heaven and pour out so much blessing that you will not have room enough for it. I will rebuke the devourer for your sake, and the vines in your fields will not cast their fruit before their time,' says the Lord Almighty. 'Then all the nations will call you blessed, for yours will be a delightful land,' says the Lord Almighty."

There is a clear progression in this passage, starting with God's command to give, followed by a promise from God, and then blessings for those who obey the Lord. It's clear that God requires His people to give Him their tithe, and if they withhold it from God, it's **robbery!**

The core issue to God is our heart attitude. Tithing is one way that God asks us, "Do you trust Me?" When you have a Godly perspective, you see that everything you own is God's. Tithing simply is a way of returning to God a portion of what He has blessed you with. In doing so, you demonstrate your thankfulness to Him for His provision and your devotion to Him in every area of your life. If you are concerned that you do not make enough money to give 10% of your income to the Lord, this is an opportunity for you to grow in your faith. Remember, God not only deserves your money, but withholding it from Him is robbery!

Don't forget the wonderful and mighty promises in Malachi! When you honor God by bringing Him your tithe, He will bless the trust you are placing in Him. God is faithful, and He will honor you for your obedience!

WHAT IS THE STOREHOUSE?

In Malachi, we are instructed to bring the tithe to the "storehouse." There is much debate about what constitutes a storehouse. I believe that in the literal sense, a storehouse is the place where PROVISION is kept for the needs of the people. When a person honors God by bringing their tithe into the storehouses, God's promise is to bless their crops. Your "crop" may be your family or a business or a job. Remember, God is faithful, and He will bless you for your obedience!

On a parallel track, I believe that your spiritual storehouse can be the Church or any ministry that is providing substantial spiritual nourishment in your life.

The Apostle Paul puts it this way to the Corinthian church: "*If we have sown spiritual things for you, is it a great thing if we reap your material things?*" (1 Corinthians 9:11). The Believers in Corinth had great material wealth, but they didn't place an appropriate value on the spiritual investment that Paul and other leaders were making in their lives.

As you grow in the Lord, ask Him to give you discernment about the ministries that are helping you grow in Christ and how you should Sow into these "storehouses."

SEED SOWING

Just because the tithe is discussed in the Old Testament doesn't mean that God only intended for it to take place in those times. No, God still requires the tithe from His people today.

Many Christians believe the lie that since tithing was taught under the Old Testament (the Law), they don't need to give God 10% of their income today. They argue that we now live under the New Testament (grace) and no longer have to honor the principle of tithing.

I wish I could share with you in this book about God's wonderful principles of giving and receiving, of Seedtime and Harvest, of living in the Covenant Promises of God and His plan to prosper you. But for now, let me just drop this "seed" into your heart. Later you can study for yourself the principles of tithing and giving in God's Word in both the Old and New testaments.

Here are a few examples for you to consider:

- Going all the way back to the earliest chapters of the Old Testament, even before God gave the Law to Moses, Abraham gave his tithe to Melchizedek, the high priest at that time (Genesis 14: 17-20).
- When God makes His Covenant with Noah never to destroy the earth again with a flood, He promises him, "*While the earth remains, seedtime and harvest...shall not cease*" (Genesis 8:22). God declares that the planting of Seeds **will** result in Harvests.
- Later in the book of Exodus, God gives the Law to Moses on Mt. Sinai where the principle of tithing is established as a law for God's people.
- Then in the New Testament, Paul reinforces this

principle of Giving and Sowing and Reaping when he writes, "*Remember this: whoever sows sparingly will also reap sparingly, and whoever sows generously will also reap generously. Each man should give what he has decided in his heart to give, not reluctantly or under compulsion, for God loves a cheerful giver. And God is able to make all grace abound to you, so that in all things at all times, having all that you need, you will abound in every good work*" (2 Corinthians 9:6-8).

In the very beginning of His Word, God establishes the principle of tithing and Seedtime and Harvest, and then He carries these principles throughout the Old and New Testaments. When you give back to the Lord a minimum of 10% of what He has given you, your gift becomes a "Seed" which you are Sowing into the Kingdom of God. God then takes this Seed and uses it to create a Harvest with which to bless your life and the lives of others! The Lord wants to use you and your resources for His work. What a privilege to partner with God.

Never give your tithes to God begrudgingly or out of resentment. Giving back to God what He has blessed you with is truly an extension of your worship and love to Him.

Remember, 2 Corinthians 9:7 says, "*Every man according as he has purposes in his heart, so let him give; not grudgingly or of necessity: **for God loves a cheerful giver.**"*

Examine your heart and your motives for giving.

When you choose to honor and obey God through your tithes, you will begin to experience God's blessings and provision in a new and exciting way!

OFFERINGS

Offerings are different from tithing; they are over and above your tithe. When you give a special offering to God, it needs to be a gift that *costs* you something. This is the concept of "sacrificial giving."

An example of this is in 2 Samuel 24. God had brought a plague against the nation of Israel because of King David's sin to number the people. Then David repented. A prophet of God came to David and instructed him to build an altar at the threshing floor owned by a man named Araunah. David came to Araunah to buy his threshing floor so he could build an altar. Araunah told King David to take everything he needed to build the altar and offer the sacrifice. Araunah bowed before David and offered to give him all the supplies the king needed for his offering. King David told him, *"I will not offer to the LORD my God burnt offerings which cost me nothing"* (verse 24). David then paid the man for the supplies and made his offering to God.

You see, offerings of worship which are meaningless to you or cost you nothing are not true worship at all. When you give an offering to God, let it be special to you . . . let it cost you something . . . let it be important and meaningful to you. This is true whether you give financially through tithes and offerings or you sacrifice your time. God knows your time is precious to you. When you take quality time out of your day to recognize Him in worship or service to others, He will not only bless you, but He will also reward you by giving more time back to you. How He does this is a mystery. From my lifelong relationship with God and through countless personal experiences, I know this is true.

WORSHIPPING GOD 24/7

Worshipping God is not something reserved only for church. On the contrary, worship is an attitude. Worship is something that you carry in your heart throughout the week. A unique way you can praise the Lord is in ordinary activities you do throughout the day. This kind of moment-by-moment connection to the Lord is what we refer to as "walking with Christ": "*Whatever you do, whether in word or deed, do it all in the name of the Lord Jesus, giving thanks to God the Father through Him*" (Colossians 3:17).

Whether you are doing housework, schoolwork, business-related work or whatever your hands find to do, do the very best you can, recognizing that you can accomplish it through God's strength. When you do this, you are actually worshipping and giving God glory, and you will be blessed and rewarded.

God's Word says, "*In Him we live and move and have our being*" (Acts 17:28). Whatever we find ourselves doing, we are to do it by the Spirit and in recognition that we are a living vessel of worship to the Lord.

When you think of God as your loving Boss, your Teacher or your Audience, you will feel an incredible motivation to do your job well. When you strive for excellence to honor God in your work, you will find yourself excelling in life, and you will be blessed: *"Commit to the Lord whatever you do, and your plans will succeed"* (Proverbs 16:3).

PRAYER

Like worship, prayer is not something that you have to approach timidly. Prayer is simply talking to God, and you can talk with Him as you would with a close friend.

Just as there are many ways to worship the Lord, there is not one specific way to pray. In fact, the Bible has many stories of individuals who prayed for many different reasons and in many different ways. Perhaps the most common image people have today of prayer is on your knees with hands folded, head bowed, and eyes closed. However, the Bible offers us many examples of how to pray.

BIBLICAL EXAMPLES OF PRAYER

The Bible says that when Daniel was at home in an upstairs room, three times a day he got down on his knees and prayed. It also says that when Daniel prayed, he gave thanks to God and asked Him for help (Daniel 6:10-11). Note that even though Daniel needed help with specific concerns in his life, he first approached God with a grateful heart. He didn't ask anything of God before he had given thanks.

Genesis 17:3 says that Abraham fell on his face before God. Abraham came to God with complete reverence and humbleness.

In Mark 11:25, Jesus told His disciples, "*Therefore I tell you, whatever you ask for in prayer, believe that you have received it and it will be yours. And **when you stand praying,** if you hold anything against anyone, forgive him, so that your Father in heaven may forgive you your sins.*" He told His followers to **stand** in faith, believing God.

Another time, Jesus lifted His eyes up to Heaven and prayed to His Father with His eyes wide open (John 11:41).

When Hannah (a godly woman in the Old Testament) went to the temple to pray, Scripture says that she was "*speaking in her heart, only her lips were moving, but her voice was not heard*" (1 Samuel 1:13). God answered her prayer for a child because of her sincerity of heart, not her posture.

However, in Psalm 142:1 David writes, "***I cry aloud with my voice** to the Lord; I make my supplication with my voice to the Lord.*"

As you can see, there is no right or wrong way to pray. You can stand or kneel, have your eyes open or shut, and speak audibly to God or talk silently to Him in your heart. Prayer is not bound by stereotype or tradition or position; just allow it to be comfortable for you and a matter of the heart.

SO WHAT DO YOU SAY TO GOD?

When you pray, tell God how much you love Him and thank Him for everything He has done for you. Worship Him. Psalm 100:4 says, "*Enter His gates with thanksgiving and His courts with praise. Give thanks to Him and praise His name.*" Thank Him for whatever makes you grateful. He is the only One worthy of praise and honor.

If you are not sure how to praise God, many of the Psalms are examples of great prayers of praise you can use to help you pray. For example, Psalm 103 is a beautiful expression of praise in which the psalmist recognizes the many things that God does for His children.

When you pray, ask the Lord to forgive you for sinful thoughts, attitudes, words, and actions. Be specific in confessing to Him what you have done wrong, and be assured that He stands joyfully ready to forgive. The Apostle John writes in 1 John 1:9, "*If we confess our sins, He is faithful and just and will forgive us our sins and purify us from all unrighteousness.*"

In Matthew 6:14, as a part of Jesus' teaching about prayer, He commands us to forgive others who sin against us. One of the greatest ways that we reflect Christ is to cultivate a merciful and compassionate heart toward others.

Beware of the devil's desires to use the shame of unconfessed sin to rob you of your peace. God is not out to punish you. Through prayers of confession, He invites you to ask for forgiveness of your own sins and also to forgive others. As you boldly approach Jesus, your

Advocate, to receive forgiveness, you will experience the restoration of pure fellowship with the Father and rekindle the joy of your salvation. Amen!

PRAYING WITH FAITH IS A MUST!

If you need guidance or direction in your life, just ask God. In James 1:5-8, we're encouraged to pursue God's wisdom in a spirit of faith:

"If any of you lacks wisdom he should ask God, who gives generously to all without finding fault, and it will be given to him. But when he asks he must believe and not doubt, because he who doubts is like a wave of the sea, blown and tossed by the wind. That man should not think to receive anything from the Lord; he is a double minded man, unstable in all his ways." God will give you wisdom when you ask; all you need to do believe!

Hebrews 11:6 tells us that anyone who comes to God must believe that He is God and that He will reward those who diligently seek Him. If you have a need in your life—in your family, your finances or your health—present it to God. The Bible says we do not have to be anxious about **anything:** *"But in everything by prayer and petition we can present our requests to God and the peace of God which surpasses all understanding will guard our hearts and minds in Christ Jesus"* (Philippians 4:6-7).

Be persistent with your prayers, and God will reward your persistence. Psalm 55:17 says, *"In the morning, noon, and in the night, continue to pray and cry aloud; and God will hear your voice.*" Do not give up; pray with consistency! "*The effectual fervent prayer of a righteous man is powerful and effective*" (James 5:16). God will reward your determination. You cannot expect a door to open without knocking first. Jesus encourages us, "*Ask and it will be given to you; seek and you will find; knock and the door will be opened unto you. For everyone who asks receives; he who seeks finds; and to him who knocks, the door will be opened*" (Matthew 7:7-8). Persistent prayer is an opportunity to express an ever-deepening hunger for God and to develop a confidence that the Lord hears your cries.

Share with your Savior about your day, and tell Him how you feel and what you need. Pray for others who need His help . . . loved ones . . . friends . . . co-workers . . . those in authority over you and over this nation . . . even your enemies. God loves to hear from you, His child, and He wants you to talk with Him about all the concerns on your heart.

This is how I often picture prayer: crawling onto the lap and into the loving arms of my Heavenly Father and with honesty and trust telling Him what's on my heart.

Spending time with God, worshipping Him and talking to Him are the most important things you can do as a new Believer, and years from now when you have grown and matured in an intimate relationship with Him. In fact, it will be our joyful occupation for all eternity!

I encourage you not to allow **anything** to interfere with your devotion times with God. Determine that you will come into His Presence to worship Him and to pray. Decide that you want to be transformed into the image of His Son, your Lord and Savior, Jesus Christ. In this way, your life will be blessed as you consistently and persistently choose His ways.

CHAPTER EIGHT

Get Involved!

Reading your Bible, worshipping the Lord, and praying are all very practical ways of feeding your spirit and strengthening your personal relationship with Jesus Christ. These are all things you can do on your own. But God knows that standing alone is not easy or healthy, and He intends for you to have support.

IN FACT, GOD HAS MADE US TO LIVE IN relationship with other Believers. This is why it's important to find a church where you can learn and grow with other Christians who believe the same way you do. Discipleship, protection, encouragement, and care come from finding fellowship with a body of Believers.

Since you have just made a decision to follow Christ, it may be likely that you do not have many Christian friends. Depending on how your family responds to your decision to serve Christ, you may feel like the only Christian in the world. If you find this to be the case, don't be discouraged! This world is filled with millions of Believers. This is one reason why going to church will encourage you. When you step into a room of people who love God just like you do, sometimes you get a small glimpse of Heaven and the joy you feel can be overwhelming.

WHY GO TO CHURCH?

God's people were instructed in the Old Testament to *"Remember the Sabbath day, to keep it holy"* (Exodus 20:8). The Sabbath day is a day of worship and rest. God knows how important church is to us, and He reminds us to attend in His Word.

Romans 10:17 says, *"Faith comes by hearing the word of God."* Where can you hear the Word of God? One obvious place is in church from the mouth of your pastor and friends. God has gifted, called, and anointed many people for leadership in churches. Those people are there to help strengthen you, guide you, and fill you up with God's teaching and His Word.

The Word of God says not to forsake assembling together with other Believers, but *"encourage one another all the more..."* (Hebrews 10:25). God wants us to feel connected to Him and to others and to be encouraged by our fellowship with people who have a common love and affection for Jesus.

In addition to offering strength, encouragement, and instruction from God's Word, getting involved in a local church will give you a chance to worship the Lord with music and songs. The Bible says, *"God inhabits the praises of His people"* (Psalm 22:3), and worshiping with other Believers can be a time of refreshment, peace, and joy as you feel the very Presence of God fill the sanctuary! Jesus said, *"Where two or three are gathered together in my name I am there in the midst of them"* (Matthew 18:20). The sweet Presence of God is welcomed into many churches every week as Christians join together to offer up their praises to Him.

Many churches have Sunday School classes. You might have attended Sunday School as a child, but it's not just for children. There are classes, Bible studies, and small fellowship groups of all sorts for adults. These can be a great time to really strengthen your knowledge and understanding of God's Word, asking mature Christians questions, and receiving feedback from the things you have studied on your own, and getting to know and ejoy other Believers.

Finding a local church can also give you an outlet for serving God with your time, talent, and treasures. God has given you abilities that may be of great help to your church. There are sure to be many areas to volunteer your services. Your church is to be an extension of your family, because they are your brothers and sisters in Christ. If they need help in an area in which you are well gifted or enjoy, pray and ask the Lord how He would like you to get involved.

The Apostle Paul says to the church in Rome, "*As we have many members in one body, but all the members do not have the same function, so we, being many, are one body in Christ and individually members of one another, having then gifts differing according to the grace that is given to us*" (Romans 12:4-6). God has given you wonderful gifts, and He delights when you use them for His glory. Simply put, the Church is most healthy when all of us are contributing our gifts for the vitality of the Body of Christ.

A piano that is not played is simply a piece of furniture. When played well, it brings the joy of song. Let God play His "melody" through your life. Pray and ask the Lord to show you ways that you can serve.

HOW DO I CHOOSE A CHURCH?

You might be saying to yourself, "How do I know which church to attend?" There are a lot of different churches today with different "labels." Which one is the right one? Some churches believe one way; others believe differently. How do you choose?

Pray! Ask God to lead and direct you to the church where He wants you to worship and serve Him. Then trust God to give you peace about where you are to worship.

Second, seek a church that believes the "whole" Bible. So many people and churches today have found it convenient or politically correct to "slice and dice" the Scripture, to pick and choose what they want to believe and "throw out" what they want to reject. The Bible says in 2 Timothy 3:16, *"**All** Scripture is inspired by God and profitable for teaching, for reproof, for correction, for training in righteousness."* It doesn't say "some Scripture;" it says, ***"all Scripture."*** The Bible also says we are not to add or take away from the words in the Bible (Revelation 22:18-19).

As much as I would like to say that all ministers of the Gospel are right in their interpretation of the Bible all the time, that just isn't so. As fallible human beings, even pastors can "miss it" at times. This is why it's important that you always ask the Holy Spirit to speak to your heart about what a particular preacher may be saying and let you know whether it lines up with God's Word or not.

You can also hear the Word of God on Christian radio stations, and on Christian television programs and networks like INSP (The Inspiration Network); i-LifeTV (Inspirational Life Television), and INI (Inspiration Network Internatioional), part of the family of networks provided by The Inspiration Networks. Here again, just because a person is on radio or television doesn't mean they speak God's truth all the time. Remember the verse that I shared earlier: *"Beloved, do not believe every spirit, but test the spirits to see whether they are from God; because many false prophets have gone out into the world"* (1 John 4:1).

SHARING YOUR FAITH

Your new-found faith in Jesus is something that God wants you to feel comfortable sharing with your family and friends, or with anyone who may ask you about being a Christian. The Bible says always to be ready to give an account for the hope that you have inside (1 Peter 3:15). People around you are sure to notice a change in your attitude, lifestyle, and behavior, so you will need to be ready to tell them why you are living so differently.

What God has done in your life is an exciting thing! You have been brought from darkness into light, and you are on your way to Heaven!

Sharing with someone what God has done in your life is called your "testimony." It's so important to testify to how God's grace and mercy have saved you, because the people you talk to may not know Jesus. With your help, they could come to the saving knowledge of Christ! How wonderful to think that someone could be in Heaven for eternity because you had the courage to share about God's grace!

Sharing your testimony is not just a nice thing to do; it is a joyful ***responsibility.*** Jesus commanded His disciples to go and tell the world about Him. Now that you know Christ died to forgive you of your sins and offer you eternal life in Heaven with Him instead of eternal hell without Him, you will want to share this good news with others. Keeping this truth to yourself is a great waste.

Could you imagine if there was a great medical breakthrough for cancer, and the doctors kept the information to themselves? So many people who would benefit from that knowledge would perish if the doctors remained silent. The truth is that the grace of God is greater news than any vaccine or cure! His salvation message is the ultimate cure for every person in this world.

SHARING THE GOOD NEWS OF THE GOSPEL

At some time, everyone's life will come to an end. However, few are willing to accept that their spirit will live forever.

Eternity is not a choice. Whether someone spends that eternity in Heaven or hell, they will spend it somewhere. Believing or not believing in eternity does not change the fact that it will come one day. Jesus has done all that He will do to make it possible for all of us to spend eternity in Heaven with Him. But He has left to us, His children, the responsibility of letting the world know this good news.

The word "Gospel" means "good news," and the Gospel is God's Word of encouragement and hope. The Bible is not only a record of history, but it also provides answers to people's struggles, and so much more.

SPECIAL DELIVERY!

When you write a letter to a friend or family member, you must place it in the hands of the post office, trusting that they will deliver it to the address you have designated. The words you wrote most likely are special and written with a purpose. What a great disappointment it would be if that letter never arrived, if the post office forgot it, or simply chose not to deliver your letter.

In the same way, God has a "letter" to be delivered to the world, and He has entrusted us with His Word and the Gospel message it contains. Like the postal carrier, we must be faithful to deliver to the world the good news about Jesus. God does not make this an option for us. We need to be prepared to share the Gospel, "*in season and out of season*" (2 Timothy 4:2).

He doesn't say, "If you remember, let your friends know who I am." He doesn't say, "If you get around to it, I would appreciate you telling your family about My Son Jesus and all He has done for them." He doesn't ask, "If it doesn't make you too uncomfortable, would you share the Gospel with your co-workers?" No, actually, He makes it very clear in His Word that we are to go and make disciples of all nations.

Before He was taken up into Heaven, Jesus told His disciples to go to all the world and make Christian disciples, baptizing them and teaching them to obey all that He told them to do (Matthew 28:19-20). This is our "Great Commission."

Please understand that this verse is not commanding you to go to the nations of the world, although God may stir within you the desire to go to a foreign country to share the Gospel with the people there. But you have your own circle of friends and family, who no one else has the ability to impact quite like yourself. These people are your priority. Once you have reached others for Christ, then they will tell others, and then they will tell others also, until the whole world is reached with the good news of Jesus Christ.

You may be saying to yourself, "I don't know enough about God and the Bible to share my faith." Well, Jesus told a Samaritan woman how she could be saved. Her life was a mess, but she gave her heart to Jesus and immediately went back to her town to tell others what Jesus had said. As a result of her testimony, *"many of the Samaritans of that city believed in Him, because of the word of the woman who testified"* (John 4:39). Isn't that amazing? She was only a Christian for a few hours, yet God used her to bring others to faith.

Don't worry about what you don't know. Like the Samaritan woman, God can use what you **do** know to lead others to Him. Rejoice that God has entrusted you with His precious Gospel; do not be afraid to share this wonderful, life-giving message with others!

And remember, you are not responsible for someone accepting Jesus as their Savior. That is the work of the Holy Spirit. Your responsibility is to share your testimony of Jesus with truth and grace.

CHAPTER NINE

Wage War

There are two spiritual forces in this world. You can think of them as light and darkness, or good and evil. Call them what you will; they are very simply God and Satan.

IN THE BEGINNING OF TIME when God created all the angels, He created them with a free will, including the choice to serve and worship Him. Lucifer was a very beautiful angel who appears to have been created to lead the worship in Heaven (Ezekiel 28:13).

One day Lucifer began to swell with pride. He wanted all the attention and adoration of Heaven, and he believed he could get it. One third of all the angels sided with Lucifer in his efforts to overthrow God and take His throne, and they turned against God, their Creator and Lord. Because of this revolt, God cast Lucifer (Satan) and the angels (demons) who followed him to an eternity of damnation and a future of destruction in the fiery pits of hell (Isaiah 14:12-15). As a result of this rebellion, Satan with his demons have been actively assaulting mankind to this day.

The truth is that God has 100% victory over Satan. Satan is already defeated. He has lost. He *will* spend eternity in hell. Satan is a liar and deceiver. His agenda is to "*kill, steal and destroy.*" Jesus, on the other hand said that He came that we might have life and have it more abundantly (John 10:10). Remember that the victory is already ours!

A SPIRITUAL BATTLE

Ephesians 6:10-12 clearly tells us that our battle is not a physical one, but a spiritual one—a battle that must be waged in the spirit realm:

"Finally, my brethren, be strong in the Lord, and in the power of his might. Put on the whole armor of God, that ye may be able to stand against the wiles of the devil. For we wrestle not against flesh and blood, but against principalities, against powers, against the rulers of the darkness of this world, against spiritual wickedness in high places."

Although this may sound like a science fiction movie, I assure you the war is very real. There is a spirit world, and it is just as real as the natural one in which you and I live. However, this spiritual realm is invisible to your eyes. Within this realm, there was a battle raging for your soul. But, God won that battle when you called on the name of Jesus! When you asked Jesus to forgive your sins and come into your heart, He did just that. Jesus now lives inside of you. God has delivered you from the kingdom and power of darkness and translated you into the Kingdom of His dear Son (Colossians 1:12-14).

THE POWER WITHIN

The Holy Spirit lives inside of you and Jesus' Blood that He shed on the Cross covers your sins. Jesus has purchased your life with His Blood, and He has deposited His Spirit within you! You are God's property, purchased at the highest possible price. One day, the Lord will return, and when He does, He will claim you as His own because of the seal of God's Holy Spirit that is upon you.

Acts 20:28 says, *"He bought the church of God with his*

own blood." Jesus paid the ultimate price by giving His life. God would never have allowed His only Son to suffer and die for a Church that would be bound by limitations. NO WAY!

You must realize that you have ***100%*** victory over the power of the enemy because of Jesus' power within you. At the very name of Jesus, all demons on earth and under the earth tremble. However, just because you are a child of God does not mean the forces of Satan will leave you alone. On the contrary, he is aggravated now more than ever because you have escaped his clutches. You were once bound with him to an eternity in hell, but now you are entitled to an abundant life and an eternity in Heaven with a loving God!

Satan will try to come against you, to tempt you, to entice you into sin, and try to deceive you. When you find the devil trying to steal your life, your family, your marriage, your job, or your finances, you need to do what James instructed Believers to do: *"Submit to God, resist the devil, and he must flee from you"* (James 4:7). Speak to Satan out loud and command him to flee in the name of Jesus. For the rest of your life, there will be spiritual battles. But never forget, God won the war with Satan when Christ paid for our sins on the Cross.

Never be afraid or intimidated by the power of the enemy, because the One Who is in you is greater than the one who is in the world (1 John 4:4).

Jesus promises us, *"Whatsoever you shall bind on earth shall be bound in heaven: and whatsoever you shall loose on earth shall be loosed in heaven"* (Matthew 18:18). In the name of Jesus, you have the power to bind the spiritual forces of darkness that come against you, your family, and the circumstances of your life—whatever they may be.

This is what spiritual warfare is all about: binding the powers of darkness in the name of Jesus Christ and by the "delegated authority" He has given us.

Delegated authority is what a local policeman carries. If his power isn't sufficient, he has the entire police department behind him. If that isn't enough, state law enforcement will back him up. And if even more might is required, the entire US military stands behind that local officer. While you may be a single new Believer, the power of the God of all eternity is behind you in every trial and in every spiritual battle you face.

VICTORY OVER SICKNESS

Once we bind principalities and powers in the spirit world, we are to "loose" the Spirit of God over the circumstances and situations we are facing (Matthew 18:18).

Let me give you an example. Suppose you are facing a physical illness. Where does sickness come from? It comes from Satan. Sickness is a result of the curse that came upon the world when Adam and Eve sinned and disobeyed God in the Garden of Eden. God never intended for us to experience sin, sickness, or death.

But when Adam and Eve used their free will to disobey God and eat of the forbidden fruit from the Tree of

Knowledge of Good and Evil, they brought a curse upon every man and woman who would ever be born. The result: sin, sickness, and death entered the world. Thank God that He did not leave us in that state! He sent His Son to suffer and die so that we could have life, not just in eternity, but here in this life, too. Jesus took upon Himself the sins of the world and paid the death penalty for man's sin.

So, what can you do?:

1. Come against the spirit of sickness and disease in the name of Jesus. By the power of the Holy Spirit, bind the spirit of sickness over your life or the life of another on this earth.

2. Ask God to bind the spirit of sickness and disease in the Heavens.

3. Release health over your life. Release the Spirit of the Resurrected Christ Who lives within you to give life to your body. Romans 8:11 says, *"But if the Spirit of him that raised up Jesus from the dead dwell in you, he that raised up Christ from the dead shall also quicken your mortal bodies by his Spirit that dwells in you."*

4. Ask God to release healing over your body. As I already noted, Jesus taught about the power we have to "bind" and "loose." He said that whatever we bind on earth will be bound in Heaven and whatever we loose on earth will be loosed in Heaven. We need to remember this Scripture!

God does not always bring a miraculous healing. Sometimes He is using our hardship to create a greater dependence on Him. Yet, I can say with confidence that everyone who knows Jesus as Savior will experience healing—sometimes it will be instant, sometimes it will be over time and ALL sickness will be eliminated in Heaven!

If you don't experience immediate healing, continue to press into the Lord and ask in faith.

YOU ARE ON THE WINNING TEAM!

Fear not. God is on your side. He is also living in you. Nothing can harm you unless you allow it to. And no hardship can come into your life that God cannot use to make you more like Jesus. The Bible reminds us,

> *"When tempted no one should say, 'God is tempting me.' For God cannot be tempted by evil, nor does he tempt anyone; but each one is tempted when, by his own evil desires, he is dragged away and enticed. Then after desire has conceived, it gives birth to sin; and sin, when it is fully grown, gives birth to death"* (James 1:13-15).

There is no temptation that can overtake you unless you give in to it.

And remember, you do not have to fight alone! If you try, you will surely fail. Paul says, *"I can do all things through* **Christ** *who strengthens me"* (Philippians 4:13).

When you find yourself being enticed, look for a way out. God promises He will always give you a way of escape. Paul writes, *"No temptation has seized you except that which is common to man. And God is faithful; He will not let you be tempted beyond what you can bear. But when you are tempted, He will also provide a way out so that you can stand under it"* (1 Corinthians 10:13).

Do not expect your way out to be displayed in flashing neon lights or for God to mysteriously transport you someplace else. Oftentimes, your way out is to boldly declare, "NO!" God will give you the strength you need to withstand temptation. It is up to you to access His strength.

You are in a spiritual war, and you must now learn how to defend yourself. Just like with any battle, it's essential to protect yourself, to put on your spiritual armor, and to pick up your weapons. The Apostle Paul uses armor and battle as a metaphor for how we guard our hearts and minds for Christ. Ephesians 6 emphatically declares:

"Our struggle is not against flesh and blood, but against the rulers, against the authorities, against the spiritual forces in the heavenly realms. Therefore, put on the full armor of God, so that when the day of evil comes, you may be able to stand your ground, and after you have done everything to stand, stand firm then. With the belt of truth buckled around your waist, with the breastplate of righteousness in place, and with your feet fitted with the readiness that comes from the gospel of peace. In addition to all this, take up the shield of faith, with which you can extinguish all the flaming arrows of the evil one. Take the helmet of salvation and the

sword of the spirit, which is the word of God. And pray in the spirit on all occasions with all kinds of prayers and requests. With this mind, be alert and always keep on praying for the saints" (Ephesians 6:12-18).

There is a war waging in the spiritual realm for your soul. When you put on the armor of God and pick up the sword of the Spirit (the Word of God) in the name of Jesus, you will stand against any foe. Don't sit back and wait for the enemy to come to you. Don't fight a **defensive war** in the spirit realm. You cannot watch passively as the enemy tears at the very fabric of your life! Get on the **offensive!** Go on the attack in the name of Jesus Christ!

SPIRITUAL WARFARE

Most of the time, spiritual battles manifest themselves in the natural world as the enemy tries to attack you or your family. When this happens, stand firm in Jesus name! Take authority over the power of the enemy!

There is no question that you are at war. The question is, "Are you willing to fight?" Jesus declares, *"The kingdom of heaven suffers violence, and the violent take it by force"* (Matthew 11:12). It's time to put on the armor of God and become spiritually aggressive with the forces attacking your life. Remember: Jesus has given us the authority to bind and loose in the earth and in the Heavenlies where spiritual battles are fought.

It's time to wage spiritual warfare through prayer.

Rebuke any spirit of darkness that comes against you or your family and bind that spirit in the name of Jesus and by His delegated authority given to you. You have been deputized!

Be specific about the point of battle. If it's an attack against you or your family, you declare to the devil, "In Jesus' name, by the power of the Holy Spirit, and the authority of God's Word, get out of my life and the life of my loved ones!" And then continue to pray. The devil doesn't give up easily, but we have the "greater power" within us. Continue to pray until you experience God's victory.

In Luke 10:19 Jesus says, *"Behold I give to you power to tread on serpents and scorpions, and over all the power of the enemy; and nothing shall by any means hurt you."*

You no longer have to handle life's struggles and problems in your own strength. Don't even try it! Rely on God's strength and power within you to defeat every power of the enemy.

Sometimes your problems may be intangible. You might feel a spirit of depression, oppression, or loneliness pressing in on you. Fight these spirits in the same way. Call their name out and bind them in the name of Jesus Christ. Speak God's promises in the Scriptures out loud over yourself. Fight for your life; do not give up! When you are weak, the Lord will be your strength. The devil will come against you, but he cannot harm you! You are a child of God!

CHAPTER TEN

The Return of Christ

*D*eath could not hold our Savior.
He went to the depths of hell
and tore the keys of death
and the grave from Satan.
On the third day,
Jesus rose again.

AFTER JESUS ROSE FROM THE DEAD, He lived with His disciples on this earth for 40 days teaching, preaching, and proving that He was who He claimed to be— Jesus Christ, the Son of the living God!

This single factor is what sets Christianity apart from every other religion. You see, all other gods died and are still dead. Not a single one of them could do what Jesus did for us. Not one of them conquered death and the grave and offered the way to true life.

JESUS IS PREPARING A HOME FOR YOU!

When it was time for Jesus to return to Heaven, He didn't leave this world through death. He ascended into the clouds and was taken to Heaven before His disciples' eyes (Acts 1:9).

Before He died, Jesus made a promise to them in John 14:1-4: *"In my Father's house there are many mansions; if it were not so, I would have told you. I am going to prepare a place for you, I will come back and take you to be with me that you also may be where I am. You know the place where I am going."*

Then Thomas, one of Jesus' disciples, asked Him how they could know where He was going so that they could be sure to get there, too. Jesus answered, *"I am the Way the Truth and the Life. No one comes to the Father except through me"* (John 14:6). Following Jesus is the only way to life.

ONLY ONE WAY!

Jesus told His disciples that He was going to Heaven to prepare a place for them, and that one day He would come back and take them to be with Him. One day Jesus is returning to earth for the Church, His "Bride," and bring us to Heaven to live forever. Until that day, we are to follow the Way that was made clear. There is only one Way to Heaven, and it's through Jesus Christ. So many people stumble over Jesus as the only means of salvation. Instead, they should be thrilled that God has provided a Way at all. Praise God for His marvelous provision for those of us who trust in Jesus!

THE "LAST DAYS"

When you hear people talking about the "Last Days," the "Second Coming," and the "Rapture" of the Church, they are referring to the day that Jesus will return. No one knows the exact day or the hour, but we do know that God is faithful to His Word, and one day our Savior will return as He promised.

Christ's return will not be like His first coming when He was born and placed in a humble manger. His return will be in Heavenly glory with trumpet sounds as He comes victoriously for His children. The Apostle Paul talks about this day in 1 Thessalonians 4:16-17: "*For the Lord Himself will come down from heaven, with a loud command, with the voice of the Archangel and with the trumpet call of God, and the dead in Christ will rise first.*

After that, we who are still alive and are left will be caught up together with them in the clouds to meet the Lord in the air. And so we will be with the Lord forever."

Paul goes on to encourage us to "comfort one another" with this good news. I know life can be hard at times, but it's important that we cultivate an eternal perspective, looking to our future "homecoming" with such eagerness that we find comfort and strength to live well for Jesus right now!

Paul assured his readers in the rest of his letter to the Thessalonians that the coming of the Lord is not a day to be feared. In verse 9 and 10 of the same chapter he states, *"For God did not appoint us to suffer wrath but to receive salvation through our Lord Jesus Christ. He died for us so that, whether awake or asleep, we may live together with Him."* Paul urges his readers not to become so obsessed with the Second Coming of Christ that they forget to live for today.

As Christians, we surely are excited for the day that our Lord will return. Until then, it's important to live as Paul explained in verse 8: *"Let us be self-controlled, putting on faith and love as a breastplate, and the hope of salvation as a helmet."* We should live each day to the fullest. We are never promised tomorrow, so always share the light and love of Christ until we hear that trumpet sound!

BE BLESSED AND BE A BLESSING

The angels in Heaven are surely rejoicing over your salvation, and I join them with thanksgiving for you! What an exciting life you have stepped into! There are so many wonderful blessings that await you, not only in this life, but also in the life to come. I hope this book has helped open a door that shows you what it means to have a personal, intimate relationship with Jesus Christ, what it means to be "born again," and what Christianity is all about.

I have tried to explain some basic spiritual truths the Bible holds. I know you can appreciate how each heading or chapter in this book could have been a separate book. But, this was not my intent. I simply want this book to help your personal relationship with the Lord Jesus Christ get started in the right direction.

No matter what happens in your life, remember always to trust in the Lord. He will never leave you nor forsake you. God is a faithful God. He has brought you this far, and He will see you through!

My friend, as you begin your new walk with Christ, I pray that . . .

- The light of Christ's love shines so brightly through you that no one will be able to deny the difference in your life.
- You overflow with the joy of the Lord and learn to draw strength from Him.
- His unsurpassable peace fills your heart and your mind at all times.
- You learn to rest in His amazing grace and be refreshed by His mercy each morning.
- You learn to trust God's hand for guidance and look to Him for direction in your life.
- You be filled with the power of the Holy Spirit.

- You hunger and thirst for righteousness.
- You walk with Christ daily, living a life that draws others toward Him.

Press on, my dear friend, to win the prize to which God has called you. Shine your light brightly so that all may see Christ in you. And one day, you will stand before your Lord Jesus in Heaven and hear the marvelous words of your Savior and Friend, *"Well done my good and faithful servant, enter into the joy of your Master"* (Matthew 25:21)! Amen.

Barbara (my wife) and I and the ministry staff at The Inspiration Networks welcome the opportunity to agree with you in prayer over any needs you may have in your new life in Christ.

Please call, write, or email to let us know how we can pray for you or serve you as you continue to grow in Jesus.

Always remember...

We Are Here For You!

David

Inspiration Ministries
P.O. Box 7750
Charlotte, NC 28241
1-704-525-9800
www.inspiration.org

Scriptures to Encourage You

OVER THE YEARS, I've found that Scripture memorization helps strengthen my confidence in the Lord, my confidence in spiritual battle, and my effectiveness in living for Christ daily. I encourage you to memorize the following verses over the next several months. Learning one new verse a week would be a great goal! You'll be amazed at how God will strengthen you as His Word gets inside your heart and mind.

ASSURANCE OF SALVATION:

Romans 10:9—*"If you confess with your mouth Jesus as Lord, and believe in your heart that God raised Him from the dead, you will be saved."*

1 John 5:12—*"He who has the Son has (eternal) life; he who does not have the Son of God does not have the life."*

Romans 6:23—*"For the wages of sin is death, but the free gift of God is eternal life in Christ Jesus our Lord."*

THE POWER OF THE WORD:

2 Timothy 3:16-17—*"All Scripture is inspired by God and profitable for teaching, for reproof, for correction, for training in righteousness, so that the man of God may be adequate, equipped for every good work."*

Psalm 119:11—*"Your word have I treasured in my heart, that I may not sin against You."*

FORGIVENESS:

1 John 1:9—*"If we confess our sins, He is faithful and righteous to forgive us our sins and to cleanse us from all unrighteousness."*

Psalm 103:12—*"As far as the east is from the west, so far has He removed our transgressions (sins) from us."*

COMFORT AND PEACE:

Philippians 4:6-7—*"Be anxious for nothing, but in everything by prayer and supplication with thanksgiving let your requests be made* known to God. And the peace of God, which surpasses all comprehension, will guard your hearts and your minds in Christ Jesus."

John 14:27—"Peace I leave with you; My peace I give to you; not as the world gives do I give to you. Do not let your heart be troubled, nor let it be fearful."

PRAYER:

Hebrews 11:6—"He is a rewarder of those who seek Him."

Luke 18:1—"At all times they (men) ought to pray and not to lose heart."

Philippians 4:6-7—"Be anxious for nothing, but in everything by prayer and supplication, let your requests be made known to God; and the peace of God, which surpasses all understanding, will guard your hearts and minds through Christ Jesus.

TRUST:

Proverbs 3:5-6—"Trust in the LORD with all your heart and do not lean on your own understanding. In all your ways acknowledge Him, and He will make your paths straight."

Romans 8:28—"We know that God causes all things to work together for good to those who love God, to those who are called according to His purpose."

VICTORY:

Romans 8:37—"In all these things we overwhelmingly conquer through Him who loved us."

I John 5:4-5—"This is the victory that has overcome the world—our faith. Who is the one who overcomes the world, but he who believes that Jesus is the Son of God?"

WORSHIP:

Psalm 34:1,3—"I will bless the LORD at all times; His praise shall continually be in my mouth. Oh, magnify the LORD with me, and let us exalt His name together."

Psalm 95:6-7—"Come let us worship and bow down, let us kneel before the LORD our Maker. For He is our God, and we are the people of His pasture and the sheep of His hand."

Psalm 16:11—"In Your presence is fullness of joy; in Your right hand are there pleasures forevermore."

Glossary

Abba—a term of affection for God, literally meaning "daddy."

Advocate—a legal term, referring to one who pleads the cause of another; in the case of salvation, Jesus is our Advocate, who testifies to His Father on our behalf that we are without guilt, because of our trust in Him for salvation.

Angels—spirit beings who serve God in worship, carry special messages, and bring protection and assistance to God's people.

Anointed—to set apart or consecrate for holy or sacred use; Jesus is the "Christ," which literally means "anointed one."

Atone—to cover or to cleanse; reconciling man to God through the Blood of Jesus Christ, which covers our sins.

Baptism—a sacrament that symbolizes the new Christian's death to the old sin-life and his new birth in Christ. It also signifies public declaration or identification with Jesus as Lord.

Believer—one who finds salvation by faith alone, through grace alone, by Christ alone.

Body of Christ—the larger Christian community and all those around the world who are a part of it.

Born Again—to experience a spiritual rebirth, where we literally pass from spiritual condemnation (because of our sin) into eternal life because we confess with our mouth and believe in our heart that Jesus is Lord. When we are born again, the Holy Spirit breathes new life into our spirit: Christ is born in us spiritually.

Christianity—the relationship of people to Christ, made up of teachings of Christ and recorded by the writers of the Scriptures.

Church—the universal community of followers of Christ.

Covenant—a holy, eternal promise or contract between God and man. Jesus secures the Covenant that ensures eternal salvation to those who place their trust in Him.

Day of Christ Jesus—the day when Jesus will return to earth to take His followers home to Heaven with Him.

Demons—evil spirits; angels who were cast out of Heaven when they sided with Lucifer in his rebellion against God.

Disciple—someone who accepts the views of a teacher and adheres to those teachings; we are "disciples" of the teachings of Jesus Christ and of the entire Bible.

Faith—the belief that something is true for which there is no proof. In the spiritual realm, we believe by faith in a God we cannot see. On a practical level, faith is simply responding in obedience to what you believe is God's will for your life.

Fellowship—to gather together with other Believers; most commonly refers to mutual times of worship and celebration.

Glory—the splendor, honor, brightness, praise, distinction, and majesty of God; His infinite perfection.

Gospel—the "good news" that Jesus is the Way of salvation to all who believe.

Grace—God's undeserved mercy, favor, power, and blessing toward all who believe in Jesus as Savior.

Great Commission—the call of God on the lives of all Believers to tell others about salvation in Jesus.

Heir—a person who is entitled to inherit property, possessions, or benefits from someone who wants to give something special to that person. We inherit salvation, the blessings, and promises of God, and ultimately, eternal life in Heaven because we are "heirs" along with Christ.

Holy of Holies—the innermost part of the Temple where the ark of God was placed and where His presence resided on earth. It was the place the high priest would experience the Presence of God and bring an offering to make atonement for the sins of the people.

Holy Spirit—the third person of the Trinity. He empowers, teaches, comforts, and convicts us of sin. He is equal to God the Father and God the Son.

Jehovah Jirah—the Lord God is our "provider"

Jehovah Rapha—the Lord God is our "healer"

Jehovah Shalom—the Lord God is our "peace"

Lamb's Book of Life—a book in which the names of all God's children are recorded; on the Day of Judgment, all those whose names are in this book will enter into Heaven for eternity.

Lucifer—literally, the "morning star"; Satan's name before being cast out of Heaven by God for his rebellion.

Offerings—special gifts that we present to God in addition to our tithes.

Parable—stories or illustrations from everyday life that Jesus used to teach a spiritual lesson.

Prayer—conversation with God that often includes worship, request for personal forgiveness, and requests for both personal needs and the needs of others.

Repentance—a turning away from our sin; literally a renouncement, an about-face from sin to an embracing of God's ways; a change of mind.

Resurrection—to be raised from the dead; most significantly, when Jesus was raised from the dead after He was crucified on the Cross and buried in a tomb.

Righteous—holy; when we accept Jesus as Savior and Lord, we exchange our sin for Jesus' righteousness; we are, in essence made in "right standing" with God when we are saved.

Sabbath—a special day of rest, given by God to man. Also called the "Lord's Day"—a time set aside for worship and rest.

Salvation—the process of being saved by Jesus death and our trust in His sacrifice as our only way to gain acceptance with God and be set free from our sin and shame.

Satan—the devil; God's evil enemy, and the enemy of every Believer.

Savior—Jesus, Who is the only way we can be saved from sin and death.

Scripture—another term that refers to the Bible, God's revealed will to His children, and written by men under the power of the Holy Spirit.

Second Coming—when Jesus will come back to earth a second time to judge mankind and to take His followers to Heaven forever.

Sins—disobedience to God.

Spiritual Warfare—fighting against the spiritual forces of darkness by the power of the Holy Spirit and the authority of God's Word.

Temptation—enticement to do something wrong.

Testimony—telling others how much God loves us and what He has done for us.

Tithe—giving one-tenth of your income to God's work.

Trinity—the three distinct persons of God—God the Father, God the Son, and God the Holy Spirit. One of the great mysteries of the faith is that they are one, separate, and equal all at the same time.

Word of God—another term that refers to the Bible, a collection of 66 individual books, written by prophets, priests, and apostles under the leadership of the Holy Spirit.

Worship—expressing devotion and adoration to God.

About the Author

DAVID CERULLO has a vision to impact people for Christ worldwide through media and has combined his strong business skills with his passion for ministry to fulfill his God-given mission.

He has established *INSPIRATION MINISTRIES*, an international media ministry based at the City of Light in South Carolina, that reaches out to more than 1.2 billion Souls in over 120 nations with the Gospel of Jesus Christ through three different television networks.

Having achieved national and international recognition as a television broadcaster and religious leader, David is a member of the National Cable Television Association, the Cable and Telecommunications Association for Marketing, the National Association of Television Program Executives, and has served on the Board of Directors for the National Religious Broadcasters Association.

David and his wife, Barbara, host a popular daily television program, *"INSPIRATION TODAY!"* They have been married for more than 36 years and have two adult children and five grandchildren.

Visit their website at **www.inspiration.org** to receive teaching from the Word, ministry updates, or to request prayer.

Inspiration PROMISE BOOK

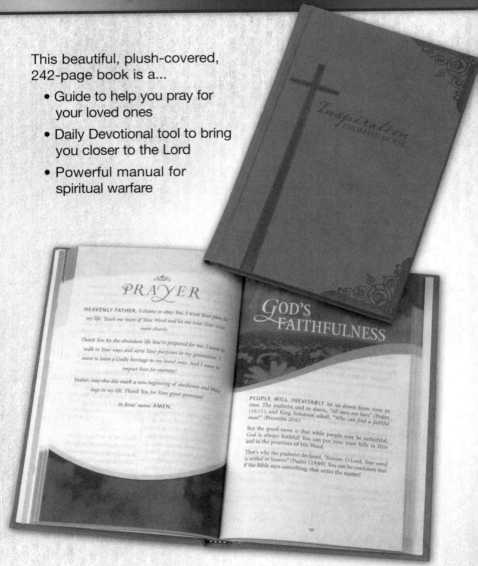

This beautiful, plush-covered, 242-page book is a...

- Guide to help you pray for your loved ones
- Daily Devotional tool to bring you closer to the Lord
- Powerful manual for spiritual warfare

PRAYER

HEAVENLY FATHER, I choose to obey You. I trust Your plan for my life. Teach me more of Your Word and let me hear Your voice more clearly.

Thank You for the abundant life You've prepared for me. I want to walk in Your ways and serve Your purposes in my generation. I want to leave a Godly heritage to my loved ones. And I want to impact lives for eternity!

Father, may this day mark a new beginning of obedience and blessings in my life. Thank You for Your great promises!

In Jesus' name, AMEN.

GOD'S FAITHFULNESS

PEOPLE WILL INEVITABLY let us down from time to time. The psalmist said in alarm, "All men are liars" (Psalm 116:11), and King Solomon asked, "Who can find a faithful man?" (Proverbs 20:6).

But the good news is that while people may be unfaithful, God is always faithful! You can put your trust fully in Him and in the promises of His Word.

That's why the psalmist declared, "Forever, O Lord, Your word is settled in heaven" (Psalm 119:89). You can be confident that if the Bible says something, that settles the matter!

Visit **www.inspiration.org**, or call 866-324-5001 to Sow a See ministry resources as a "Thank You" gift for partneri

BE BLESSED!

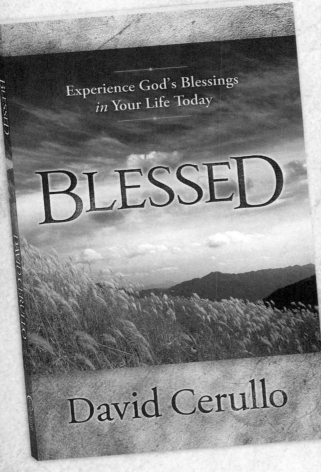

Experience God's Blessings in Your Life Today

BLESSED

David Cerullo

God wants to bless you abundantly! My latest book, ***Blessed***, provides you with...

- 12 life-changing "Blessing Keys"
- A simple equation to release God's abundance
- Fresh insights on God's powerful principles of Seedtime and Harvest

"I will bless you...and you shall be a blessing."
–GENESIS 12:2

r Souls and receive one or more of these life-changing
ith us to impact people for Christ worldwide!